10/05

his oldest friend

his oldest friend

the story of an unlikely bond

. . .

Sonny Kleinfield

TIMES BOOKS

henry holt and company | new york

Times Books
Henry Holt and Company, LLC
Publishers since 1866
175 Fifth Avenue
New York, New York 10010

Henry Holt® is a registered trademark of
Henry Holt and Company, LLC.

Library of Congress Cataloging-in-Publication Data

Kleinfield, Sonny.
His oldest friend : the story of an unlikely bond / Sonny Kleinfield.—1st ed.
    p.   cm.
ISBN-13: 978-0-8050-7580-9
ISBN-10: 0-8050-7580-1
1. Oliver, Margaret, 1910–   2. Checo, Elvis, 1983–   3. Nursing home
patients—New York (State)—New York—Biography.   4. Older women—
New York (State)—New York—Biography.   5. Immigrants—New York (State)—
New York—Biography.   6. Dominicans (Dominican Republic)—New York
(State)—New York—Biography.   7. Intergenerational relations—New York
(State)—New York.   8. Manhattan (New York, N.Y.)—Biography.   I. Title.
CT275.O466K55   2005
305.26'2'092—dc22   2005043084

Henry Holt books are available for special promotions and
premiums. For details contact: Director, Special Markets.

First Edition 2005

Designed by Kelly S. Too

Printed in the United States of America
1   3   5   7   9   10   8   6   4   2

his oldest friend

· *1* ·

Late in the afternoon, the old woman knew to look for him.
Four o'clock. Their time. In readiness, she turned off the TV,
stabbing at the buttons on the remote with her unreliable
arthritic fingers. The detergent commercial on the screen
dissolved into blackness. She felt okay, she thought. Her
door was open, and she waited for him at the other end of
the tidy antiseptic room in the nursing home, her posture
upright in the wheelchair, her bag of paraphernalia fastened
behind her. The pillow on her bed was winsomely inscribed,
"If things get better with age, then I'm approaching magnifi-
cence." A slash of sun danced on the far wall. It was warm,
and there was a balmy wind. She had the windows shoved
up as far as they would go, which was not all that far. Regula-
tions. As she liked to say, "I guess they're worried we'll jump
out. I suppose some of us might."

Her roommate was AWOL, as she usually was during the day, routinely rolled out to perch in the buffed dining area, seeing the comings and goings. She had a persistent blank expression on her face, the telltale look of dementia. You could talk to her and she might talk back, but it would not be a conversation. Day after day, she tirelessly mumbled to herself—"Why am I here?" "This place—where is anybody?" The old woman sometimes woke up to these plaintive summonses, starting her day a bit earlier than she had intended, a bit more cacophonous than she had intended.

Almost right on the dot, the young man strode into her room. Oversized jeans shorts sliding off his hips, a T-shirt expansive as a nightgown nuzzling his knees—yes, it was him, all right. Four o'clock. Their time.

"Hey, Miss Oliver," he said in a low offhand voice. "How you doing? Allstate is here." That was one of their little jokes, him reassuring her by telling her, "You're in good hands with Allstate."

"Hi, Elvis. I'm doing okay."

He always called her Miss Oliver. She called him Elvis. In the hood where he lived he was often known as "El" or "EC" or "Easy E" or sometimes "Evicious," this last nickname because he was small but had a reputation for being vicious when someone ragged on him. He grew up in a rambunctious culture where if you let someone push you around, you were considered a coward. He was no coward.

He gave her that big megawatt smile. Her vision was

middling to poor—glaucoma fouling her eyes—and from a distance she could barely see him, couldn't even tell if he was smiling or scowling. But she knew his voice as well as her own. She could walk a little, but not much, and so she rode her wheelchair most of the time.

She was near the window. She looked really nice today. Next to her on her nightstand were piled large-print books from the home's library that she was plowing her way through, along with a partly filled pitcher of water and a box of tissues. No big worries today, just routines. It had been a day down at rehab for some paraffin wax on her crippled hands, a leisurely session of bingo, a little reading in her Agatha Christie mystery, and then the TV, shows flickering one after the other, some good, some dreadful, many boring. She finished up watching the BBC, her afternoon fare. She liked that channel, liked the way it presented the world's news better than the American networks, which were too much entranced with tragedy and pathos. She had exchanged just about no words with anyone.

"Should we go to the dayroom?" he asked her.

"Absolutely," she said, her response alert and precise. "But see if I have my sweater behind me. It can get cool there."

There was a time when the old woman had played tennis, traveled the world, made clothes with the nimble hands of an expert seamstress. How she had liked to get out, see the opera, go to the theater. Now she lived her life on a few major fronts: the television, books, the day's activities in the auditorium, and conversations with her assorted visitors. Her life had become assigned to this home of the old and infirm. It was where she would be until the end, this place of too many sorrows, the final corner of her universe. She was okay with this, this daily chase after self-respect. It had been almost two years. Unlike so many of her cranky neighbors, she had achieved a negotiated peace with old age and with the home, the litany of shalts and shalt-nots, her life put in a new alignment. Sometimes the nursing home staff would try to manufacture some version of youth, like when they held "dances" where attendants would twirl the wheelchairs around the auditorium, but she didn't go for that. She went and watched, but she knew what real dancing was and she had accepted the fact that she would not do it again. When you get old, life gets smaller—what's for breakfast, time for meds, let's see what's on *Oprah*—and she was content with smaller. She didn't see that she had much choice.

After gently draping her sweater over her shoulders, the young man steered the old woman down to the familiar territory of the dayroom on the ground floor. She liked to sit and watch the resolute motion of the passersby out the window. It injected some variety into the slow ebb and flow of her life.

He shot a quick glance around the room. Busy. All the regulars were here. Some recognized him, the ones who could still recognize. Hi. Hi.

Good spots facing the windows were prized and hard to come by. There was a wall of windows facing the street, upholstered chairs, two vast fish tanks full of aquatic exotica, a slightly battered piano. A pair of upholstered sofas bisected the space. The carpet was recently vacuumed, spotless. The sun was almost gone outside, the sky gauzy, the air getting chillier.

A heavy-lidded woman with lumpy blue veins kept up a constant patter with the younger woman attending her, accosting her with questions she didn't actually want answered: "Why is the weather so cold all the time? Why that? And are you going to get me the juice? I think I should have some juice. Something to drink. What about a shot of whiskey; how about that?" The attendant paid little attention to this extemporaneous monologue, showing not even detached curiosity.

One of the residents, a jazz musician, liked to play the piano, a worn baby grand. He had lost one of his legs. Then the other got infected, and that was amputated as well. He continued to come down and play. He played beautifully, the evidence of genuine professional talent, but the old woman could always tell something was off, because he couldn't press the pedals anymore. Stuff like that, you heard it all the time in homes.

Now another resident sat down at the piano. Gnawing at her lip, she flailed away, unable to summon the right notes. She was a good-looking woman for her age, an expectant look on her face. Hard as she rummaged through her memory, she could not find the melody, not even close. It was rough on the ears.

The old woman winced and looked doubtful. She leaned over and said to the young man, "My grandmother used to say, 'You spend a lifetime learning, and then you forget it all.'"

He wrinkled his face and said, "Maybe I should just skip some of the remembering."

She chuckled and glanced at him open-faced. Her smile was very happy. Yes, that sounded right, just skip some of the remembering.

His name was Elvis Checo. He was twenty. The old woman was Margaret Oliver. She was ninety-three.

Once he had arranged her by the windows and pulled up a chair for himself, he read her mail for her: opera news, minutes from the latest Resident Council meeting, jokes her daughter Joyce had culled from the Internet. She saved the mail until he came so they could share it. She didn't get a lot of mail.

"How about some jokes?" he asked.

"Fine, I'd like that," she replied.

He unfolded the sheet and read them to her, proceeding from page to page, getting them both chortling. They were the only ones in the dayroom laughing, and that was how it often was. He whisked through a sequence about the meaning of maturity.

"As I've matured, I've learned that one good turn gets most of the blankets."

"As I've matured, I've learned to not sweat the petty things and not pet the sweaty things."

"As I've matured, I've learned that I don't suffer from insanity, I enjoy it."

She mentioned that something happened the other day that amused her, and Elvis said, "Okay, let's have it." She said, "This guy rolled up to a nurse and asked, 'Do you have any Viagra?' The nurse replied, 'Why do you want that?' He told her, 'Well, you never know, you never know.' And he rolled away."

Not batting an eyelash, Elvis said, "Here's a joke about Viagra. A man in his seventies was playing with this little girl in the park. This woman passes and says to the daughter, 'That's so nice, you're playing with your grandfather.' The girl says, 'That's not my grandfather, it's my father.' 'Your father?' the woman says. 'He must be in his seventies.' 'Yes, he's seventy-one.' 'What's your name?' the woman says. And she says, 'Marla Viagra.'"

Ms. Oliver chuckled appreciatively.

He folded up the paper with the jokes and slipped it into the pouch hooked to the back of her wheelchair. He plucked at some lint on his voluminous jeans shorts and studied his sneakers.

She turned to the window, caught in contemplation. She knew a lot. She couldn't sit there and tell you why Saturn had rings, and, goodness knows, she couldn't explain chaos theory, how a wasp fluttering its wings in Angola could prompt a snowstorm in South Dakota. There was no way she could put a rest to the puzzle of the grassy knoll. But she had stored up a lot of wisdom about life, knowing nothing better than that life was a million riddles. A bus moaned its way down the street in the day's perishing light.

She changed the subject. She asked Elvis about his diet. She was a stalwart believer in eating the right mix of food, often pontificated to him about his meals. Her hands shook with a tiny tremor.

"I'm trying to do what you say," he said. "I'm kind of watching my diet."

Ms. Oliver pressed him about whether he was exercising.

"No, but I will," he promised. "I'm going to swim."

She said, "I always tell young people, live right, because in your old age it will tell on you."

"Yeah, I hear you. It catches up with you, huh?"

In the future he would find out what she knew, that getting old didn't take anything, no skill at all; you just kept waking up, and it happened.

"You're making good progress in living right, I can see that," she said.

"Yeah, well, I'm trying. The way I look at it, my childhood ended at nine years old when I got on an American Airlines plane from the Dominican Republic. I remember I didn't

know much. When they served the meal, I put the salad dressing on the little dessert cake. I didn't know. It actually tasted good. I had to ask what the salt packages were. I had never seen them."

"Do you miss the Dominican Republic?"

"Yes, I do. I haven't quite adapted to the routines of this country. I miss the way my country smelled. The country smells like the scent in a hot place after it rains and you smell the humidity coming out from the ground. Yes, I miss that."

The dinner hour approached, and so began the loquacious crawl of wheelchairs leaving. Dinner, the evening's centerpiece, was served at 5:30, always 5:30. Early to eat, early to bed, early to rise.

Her roommate's phone was ringing when they got upstairs. Why did that woman even have a phone—she didn't know to answer it and couldn't make sense on it—and who could be calling her other than a wrong number or one of those direct marketer nuisances? She got them too—soliciting her for charge cards and charitable contributions and luxury time-shares in the Poconos. One caller the other day pushed hard a low-interest-rate credit card, and she pointedly said, "Listen, I live in a nursing home, and I'm ninety-three. I don't think I'm what you're after." And then there was that obscene call. Ms. Oliver couldn't believe the filth she was hearing. The caller got around to inquiring if

she wanted to have sex. Without hesitation, she announced, "No, I'm a lesbian," and that shut him up. End of conversation. She got a kick out of telling that one.

"How about a Chunky and some ginger ale?" he asked her.

She smiled. "Why, Elvis, I thought you'd never ask."

It was one of their small, repeatable pleasures. She was cursed with a powerful sweet tooth, which she especially liked to satisfy with a Chunky. Ginger ale was her preferred beverage. So they liked to conclude their visits with a Chunky and a glass of ginger ale, a little appetizer before dinner that put them both in good moods.

He broke the Chunky into pieces small enough for her to manipulate. As they ate, savoring each bite, he dabbed away the chocolate smears on her face.

"How's that Chunky?" he asked her.

She said, "One of the best I've ever had."

· 2 ·

His room was in an apartment in Washington Heights, on West 179th Street. It was largely a Spanish-speaking neighborhood, in the upper reaches of Manhattan, a dystopian enclave better known for its audacious failures than for its successes. It was not a good room, and it was not a good apartment building, and it was not a good neighborhood. He took it because it was all that he could afford. Someday he hoped to get out. Right now, though, the arithmetic of his life was poor.

On the bed in his cold little box of a room, lying back after hacking into his fist, the stale air getting to him, he contemplated the chattering characters on the small television set, the only piece of furniture he could call his own. He waved the remote at the screen, hiking up the volume. Working through the channels, he settled on some cable comedy, making little sense, a man and a frizzy-haired woman babbling to each other; made you wonder how these shows ever got on the air. Outside, under a starless sky, the moon a sliver, he could hear whistling and car horns. Loud voices, raucous street noises, even in the lethargy of the night. It was a summer evening.

Elvis was compact, solidly built, his hair cropped short in what was known as a Caesar, a haircut named for the Roman ruler and popularized by George Clooney on *ER*. He had small, narrow eyes, a light stubble of beard, a timpanic voice. Tattoos adorned the inside of his arm and his wrist.

He had been at the home. Long day, weary from rolling wheelchairs. Hard to focus on the future when you're tired. He was trying to right himself, his objective too often the next meal or the week's rent, always afraid he might slip and become one more of his countrymen on the road to nowhere.

His backstory, well, it was short and hard, and when he would tell it so much of it would revolve around a meal truck parked at the curb, food sizzling inside, answering ravenous appetites, the whole thing driving him crazy.

But it would start with how he was born in 1983 in Santiago in the Dominican Republic and how his father walked out on his mother and his older brother Ronny and him when he was two years old. He didn't have a single memory of his father, had no thoughts of him. His family was poor. His father, Romeo, didn't stay much in touch, because he went off and started a new family with another woman. Romeo was a plumber, but the little money he made went to the new family. He developed a hernia that he never had the resources to get repaired, and being a plumber with a hernia in the Dominican Republic was not a combination that worked especially well.

Her marriage dissolved, Elvis's mother, Janette, began doing housecleaning, and she washed clothes for other families for almost no money, doing what she could to rummage together an income. Washing machines were unknown in his neighborhood, so she had to do it all by hand. She even did laundry for some local cops, and he would see police uniforms lying around. She also sold numbers tickets. Elvis didn't know if it was legal. He did know that there weren't too many rules in the Dominican Republic, not that he could see.

Life seemed to go on in one direction, and wherever the finish was, it seemed unlikely it would be different from the start. The family was always short of food. He often drank sugar water instead of milk or juice. He remembered liking the taste. His mother was constantly joking about something missing. If they had the meat, they didn't have the rice to go with it. If they had the rice, they didn't have the meat. Even on the best days, something was missing, and he couldn't remember a time when a meal was truly satisfying.

For years, Elvis never got a Christmas present, because his mother couldn't afford it. He recalled one toy, a police car. Someone stole it. He and his friends made toys. They would grab four buttons, two toothpicks, and a matchbox and construct a car by sliding the toothpicks through the buttons. He and his friends played basketball with a beachball. When he was desperate for candy, as any kid would be, he and his brother and cousins would scrabble up trees and swipe fruit and lemons and sell them so they could get candy, or sometimes the money would go for a notebook or pencils.

His house had three rooms and a patio, mismatched cheap furniture. There was running water that came and went. There was electricity that came and went. You never seemed to know why. He used to think it would be marvelous to live someplace where the faucets always worked. There was no bathroom, just a latrine and shower slumped in the backyard. When he was small, he always needed to go to the bathroom in the middle of the night, and so there was a routine. He slept in a bunkbed with his brother, and his mother was curled in a bed a couple of feet away. A bedpan was kept on the floor and on the table a pitcher of water, and he would infallibly wake up and use the bedpan and then take a drink of water. This woke up his mother, of course, but that was all right. One day when he was about four, he had been fooling around with his friend and stuck a pencil up his nose to look funny, and he didn't know it but a piece of the eraser lodged itself in his nostril. During the night, his mother woke up not because he used the bedpan but because he didn't, and she looked in on him and he was barely breathing. The eraser had blocked his air passage, and she rushed him to the hospital, where nurses held him down while someone pushed pliers into his nose, extracting the eraser, and, no, he never did that again.

When he was seven, his mother left for the United States with her sister, hoping to cash in on America's heralded promise. Getting to the United States sooner or later, that was what a lot of Dominicans planned on. Elvis and Ronny stayed with their grandmother, Mercedes, who was divorced and living alone, until his mother could get a footing. Elvis adored his grandmother, whom he called Tete. She really doted on him, and so that was some consolation for his mother leaving. "She would go out of her way to accommodate you," he would recall. "She would understand when a kid was impatient. I was in the street all the time, and they would make fun of me, so I fought. I fought almost every day. Over nothing. About bragging about winning a game. Or bragging about taking marbles. We played games with marbles. You'd make a hole and then a ring around it, and whoever got it in the hole after four tries won. Someone might take your marbles and make fun of you, so you fought. I won fights, and I lost some. Not to brag, I think I won most. I was a very hyper kid."

After two years, his mother sent for him and Ronny. Elvis missed his mother, but he was reluctant to leave his grandmother and his country, leave what he knew for what he didn't.

They joined her when Elvis was nine, Ronny fifteen. Maybe America was better than the Dominican Republic, but the new life was still hard. His mother had met this man in New York who was working in a food truck. Then they got married and bought their own truck. They both worked the truck, serving cooked food out in the street. Elvis helped, grilling meals in the furnace of the truck.

When he got to New York, he had to miss a year of school because there weren't enough seats. He didn't yet know English. His mother never learned. He stayed home much of the day and watched a lot of television. They only got three channels: 13, 21, and 41. He watched *Sesame Street* on channel 13, and it taught him a good deal of English. As he would say, "Lambchop helped a lot." Then he started school in an English as Second Language class and mastered it.

Things about the truck: Imagine a five-by-ten space with two stoves, a fryer, and a grill. Heat all the time. Smoke all the time. If it was 90 degrees out, it was 120 in the truck. Once he took a meat thermometer and left it out, and it climbed to 123. The only way to cool down was to get out. And standing all the time, no place to sit. He got leg cramps. He got migraines. He was always waiting for something better, something wonderful to happen, but nothing did. He had to wonder, did he just have bad luck?

Elvis's job was to make "chimis"—Dominican hamburgers. It was a popular request. Sometimes there would be thirty people lined up outside the truck. Most of them wanted chimis. People would come from Connecticut to get chimis. UPS guys would interrupt their routes to get chimis. Perhaps the greatest flattery was when they saw the workers from a nearby McDonald's shamble over on their break, still in their McDonald's outfits, and ask for one of those chimis, going with them over Big Macs.

By the division of labor, his mom did the frying. When she was frying, the oil would pop. She would be frying pig's ears, and the oil would pop. She got burns all over her arms; Elvis, standing nearby, got burns on his arms.

The only day he sometimes had off was Wednesday. Normally they would open for business at two in the afternoon. He would get out of school and cook until two in the morning. He went to bed at three, got up three hours later for school. Homework? Forget it. They would work so late, because there were always people on the street. People would be leaving clubs, and they would be hungry. Chimis, chimis.

"I hated the truck," he said. "I hate that spot where we parked. I avoid going by that space. I see it, and I get mad. I hated everything about it. Imagine a kid dealing with all those demanding people. I wanted to stab some of those people. So many were rude. They were stupid. There would be an argument every day. They'd complain we weren't fast enough. You gave me the wrong thing. They'd order something and say they didn't want that when you knew they had ordered it. There were a lot of drunks that came. One guy was mouthing off to my mom, and I went outside the truck and knocked him out. When I go to a restaurant, I always try to be as civil as I can. I always leave a good tip. I know what it's like."

He had no normal high school experience, no time to develop friendships or refine his education. There was class and the truck. Sometimes just the truck. Teachers were rarely encouraging about his potential. Most of them didn't see him developing into much. One teacher asked him what he wanted to do after college, and he said, "I don't know, I think I want to have some business, maybe go into the restaurant business." She knew he worked making chimis, and she said, "Oh, so you want to spend your life flipping burgers like your mother?" That got his back up.

He had his brother, but then something went wrong there. Ronny was in New York only eight months before he got into trouble. He didn't speak English and wasn't very popular. Bullies at school gave him a hard time. Word came down that they were going to jump him, so he grabbed his stepfather's gun (which didn't happen to be loaded) and took it to school. He was caught and suspended. His stepfather was irate and sent him back to the Dominican Republic for straightening out. This, of course, depressed Elvis. Ronny stayed there for two years, almost three. While he was there, he learned how to cut hair. He also got a girl pregnant, and she gave birth to his first child.

When Ronny returned, he ditched school and began

delivering Domino's pizzas and then cutting hair. Soon he found a girlfriend, one of an endless parade, and moved in with her. The women always went for Ronny. Sometimes he had seven or eight girlfriends at a time swooning over him. Many of them he met in the salon. When Elvis was fourteen, his stepfather returned to the Dominican Republic, and Elvis had to spend far more time in the truck. His stepfather said he needed to visit his relatives. That might have been so, but he also got mixed up with another woman and got her pregnant.

When Elvis was fifteen, his mother went to the Dominican Republic, her wrists aching from carpal tunnel syndrome from the years of work in the truck. She would awaken in the middle of the night, arousing Elvis, crying because her wrists hurt so. She wanted to get medical treatment and to look after her mother, who was ailing, and she wanted to see what was up with her man. She left Elvis behind in New York with Ronny, but with his brother adding girlfriends and children in profusion, Elvis fled to his own room. Fifteen, on his own, in the furious pace of a dangerous neighborhood, supporting himself just barely. Sometimes he went two days without eating. There was no hyperbole here; he saw his life going nowhere, a life without pride, a life on the streets without a trajectory.

His mother stayed in the Dominican Republic for two years, two very difficult years for Elvis.

When his mom left, his uncle stepped in. He had a late-night parking lot job that he wasn't crazy about. So he and Elvis started working the truck together for a couple of years. "I never did homework. Sometimes I tried to copy homework in class. I think my teachers were sympathetic, because they knew my situation. I was very hard on myself. Some classes I had to redo."

Elvis built up resentment, never able to blot out how that forlorn time felt. When his mother returned to New York, it was never the same between her and Elvis. "I don't see my mother all that much," he said. "Fortunately, our conversations are no longer only about what do we have to buy for the damned truck. For a long time I didn't forgive her for going back and leaving me here. To this day, it bothers me a lot that she hasn't apologized. That was very hard for me and had a big effect on me. I realize that it was hard for her too. So I have mixed feelings."

He wearied of the truck. He wearied of the scorching heat and the strain on his body and the ribald voices of the customers and the endless chimis. He wearied of watching his youth sacrificed to Dominican burgers. He wearied of not being given any chance to find himself, to turn himself into somebody else.

· *3* ·

They came together out of pure happenstance. You don't pick your mooring posts in life; fate delivers them. It happened like this: He was going to school downtown near Fourteenth Street, a tough school at which to see a promising future, looking to leave the despised truck. One thing he knew was not to count on anyone, because anyone he had counted on had let him down.

Classmates at school were scouting around for summer work, and he figured he had better do that, too. His life was burdensome and he needed money, but he didn't know what to do or what he wanted to do. Someone mentioned an intergenerational program operated by the New York City Department for the Aging. It offered modest remuneration for high school students willing to spend time with the elderly. He was steered to the Jewish Home & Hospital for the

Aged nursing home on West 106th Street. It had a volunteer office that relied on young people to come in and spend time with the residents, keep them company, transport them through the corridors to activities, and they never had enough recruits willing to put in the time hanging around the old. He met the volunteer director, Esperanza Jorge-Garcia, whom everyone called Espi, a woman with an immense heart who oozed goodness, and she put him to work. She believed in establishing connections between the generations, that bringing together young and old could lessen the dismissive scorn many of the elderly felt from younger generations, and it could ease the existential emptiness of old age. The young could profit from the accumulated wisdom of the elderly. They had seen some things.

The idea of sticking around for any length of time in a nursing home hadn't crossed his mind. He didn't think it would be great, but maybe it wouldn't be awful. He didn't really expect anything. Nothing. He found he didn't mind the work. In fact, he began to enjoy it. He had thought he lived in a realm inapplicable here, but then he heard the histories of Holocaust survivors, other tragedies, the sinkhole old age had become for some, and he found common ground. Everyone at the home was trying to overcome something, just as he was, and so he could become part of it, find grist for reflection as he tried to grow up. He was welcomed and appreciated, and not too often in his young life had he felt needed.

The first resident Elvis spent any time with was an old man, a stroke victim, and he used to sit with him and read him the newspaper, catching up on the blur of news and sports results. He died after a month. Gladys was the first woman he really got to know. She was lucid, but accelerating toward dementia, its ramble of words. She had a boyfriend in the home, but he died. She liked to walk up and down the hall, until she fell. Elvis would take her to the park, where they would compliment the dogs, because a lot of dogs would go by on their walks. She loved chocolate, so Elvis bought her M & M's. She was still a resident of the home, but she didn't recognize him anymore.

He used to push around a couple of men. One was ninety-five. He had a chronic breathing problem and was a bit of a grump. September 11 happened when Elvis was with him; both of them were stunned into disbelief, their own problems instantly made small and irrelevant, wholly unprepared to comprehend what would come next. Another man was a stroke victim. In a week Elvis watched him go from being okay to being unable to communicate. Now he was dead.

It wasn't long before Elvis lost what inhibitions toward the elderly he had.

Then he went through a rough patch. He dwelled too much on his mother's abandonment of him, trying to make sense of the senseless. His girlfriend of the moment was trying to prop him up, and she and her mother invited him to come live in their apartment. The place was overcrowded, full of too much commotion. There was his girlfriend, her mother, her older sister, her sister's boyfriend, her little brother, her niece, and her cat Wiggly. Elvis liked Wiggly best.

His girlfriend envisioned dropping out of high school, getting married, and having kids; she would stay home and raise the kids, and he would support her. She had a girlfriend downstairs whose life went like that, in her case the man being a drug dealer who showered her with gifts and abundant spending money. Elvis didn't see that kind of future. It didn't add up. She was promising him a love unlike any other love, but he wasn't going for it. Sensing that Elvis was distancing himself, she stopped taking her birth control pills. When she tested herself one day with a home pregnancy test kit, it came out positive. They went to a clinic, Elvis praying hard that the home test was wrong; his prayers were answered. He didn't trust her after that, making her take her pills in front of him, and in any event, his interest in her began to wane even more.

Not long after that, Elvis told his girlfriend that he was breaking things off, going to find someplace else to live. She smacked Elvis, and he hit her back, cutting her lip. He wasn't proud of that. He stood in the bathroom of his girlfriend's apartment, where a razor blade was lying on the sink. He picked it up, and some ache of humiliation compelled him to run it over his left wrist, and he began to bleed. He concealed the cut and went out.

He ran into his girlfriend, and she saw the blood, and before he knew it the police and an ambulance were there, flashing lights. The cops treated Elvis as if he had truly tried to kill himself, and it got him ten days in a mental ward. "I knew I wasn't nuts because I saw what nuts was like. There were guys biting their restraints trying to get out. Guys were biting their skin trying to get out. Guys just totally wacko."

He returned to the Jewish Home and then this crazy twist of fortune. He was lounging around with some of the others in the volunteer office on the ground floor, just past the men's room. A woman wandered in: Janet, Margaret Oliver's daughter. Her stated purpose was to find someone who would spend a few hours a week with her mother. There just wasn't enough help in the home—or in any nursing home—to do things for the woebegone residents when they wanted them done. Those with spare money, the ones who still had their wits about them, hired a "companion" to take them downstairs or tend to their mail, and if they were lucky they got a companion they could actually have a decent conversation with, someone to quiet the dark impulses.

Without hesitation, Elvis, then barely eighteen, spoke up: "I could do that."

Tentatively, she looked him over, the shaggy clothes, the tattoos.

Could this arrangement work? She guessed it would have to, and a deal was struck. The daughter agreed to pay him ten dollars an hour, money to fill his empty pockets, if he would come for an hour every Tuesday, Wednesday, and Thursday at four.

Margaret Oliver had only recently moved in, but it was actually her second time around. On her first arrival at the Jewish Home & Hospital, she was assigned to a different wing, and no one there was like her, with all her faculties, still entirely engaged with life. Her room was at the end of a hall, and all along the corridor the other residents would be lined up in their wheelchairs seemingly all day long, ranged there with dead eyes like some figures in a pantheon of lost hope. They were shades of themselves, long removed from the regular stream of life. They didn't move. They didn't talk. They didn't change their expressions. Everyone looked permanently worn out. She gazed at those people and thought she was in an insane asylum, and the strangeness of the environment disturbed her deeply. Anyone who visited her stole one look at the grim lineup and said, "Margaret, how do you stand it?" She could only look back, blank-faced.

She was someone who talked easily with anyone, people who put on airs, people who didn't, and everyone in between, and here she was faced with no one to talk to. This was not the world in which she had expected to move. Her two daughters transferred her to another home in the Bronx.

Then she learned. It was that way everywhere, and her understanding of homes underwent a substantial renovation. Nursing homes were full of not just old people but people minus their minds, and they were often freely mingled in with the others. Once you made it to eighty-five, in fact, the odds were nearly fifty-fifty, an even money bet, that dementia would claim you. The home in the Bronx was nice, all right, but the entertainment was not to her liking and the residents were the same empty shells. Her roommate was dying and would lie in bed and never speak. The aides insisted that it was important that her television always be on, and so there was a constant undercurrent of noise. The aide who attended her during the day favored the soaps and kept them going, but the aide assigned to her at night was a basketball fan and put the games on; it was just too much, listening to smooching and squabbling and then the incessant dribbling, "Yes, he hits the three!" Never in her long life had she believed in therapy, but now for the first time she wondered if she needed to talk to a therapist. The home sent one up, and she got nothing out of their session.

The answer was to leave. She returned to the Jewish Home and was assigned to a different building, where the atmosphere was somewhat better. And she adapted. She accepted what she saw as her destiny. Given enough time, you can get used to anything. Yet she knew if she was going to make it here in the unspooling months or years to come, she needed company.

The slow ticking of time was old age's exhaustive song, creating a tension that never went away. As in any nursing home, the accent was on filling the hours in an environment missing the high drama of life beyond its doors. How did you navigate the day, the week, the month, the drip, drip, drip of time? She watched TV—C-Span, the BBC, Court TV—but easily tired of the passivity of television viewing. She read, especially the intricate murder mysteries of Agatha Christie, listened to classical music and opera. There was bingo, a trivia game, lectures. Family members visited when they could: her twin daughters, Janet and Joyce, who were in their seventies; her four grandchildren; her four great-grandchildren. A few enduring friends—her old buddies Esther and Paul Abramson—came by regularly, and it was always heartwarming to see them. She went to bed at 8:30 and was up at 7:00. Still, she had time on her hands, improbable amounts of time. She tried to focus on things that could still happen, but there weren't that many. Sometimes it seemed as if there were forty-eight hours in the day.

When she met Elvis, she gave him a silent and friendly smile. He gave her a big smile back. But she wondered, What would a teenager want with her—someone rolling around in a wheelchair, who relished opera, who didn't use a computer, who couldn't even get the infernal remote control to work? She knew how society, especially the young and robust, dismissed the old and saw them as some sort of nuisance or as human pets—give them their medications and spoon-feed them their meals and then put them to bed with a pat on the head. No one seemed to believe there was anything worth learning from the elderly. Their human worth got diminished with every passing day, as if by some immutable

law. And young people, the heroes of a youth-worshipful society, just wanted to forget there was something called old age.
Rarely did you see many young men and women inside the
home, and those you did had those anxious get-me-out-of-
here looks.

Elvis was thinking something altogether different. He
wondered, What would an old woman want with him—a
moody teenager from another part of the world still trying to
decipher girls, who relaxed with video games and rap music,
who liked to toss down a few beers with the guys? What
could they talk about?

Yet Ms. Oliver felt the glow of Elvis. He made a strong
impression. Those liquid eyes, that enchanting smile. Best
of all, he didn't treat her like some dithering fossil, but as a
friend. And Ms. Oliver was the flip side of what Elvis imagined. She didn't look on him as a spacey drudge. She was
fun. He could even tell her risqué jokes, and she would
laugh uproariously.

He liked how easy she was to talk to, unlike anyone else
he had encountered at the home. She saw beyond his young
age. He would say, "When you come to a place like this as a
teenager, you feel the elderly aren't going to have any interest
in you. You're not going to have anything in common. They'd
think, Oh, he's just some young kid; who can imagine what
he's into? When you're a teenager, what you think about the
elderly is this person is old—old-fashioned, old body, old
attitude, old. Doesn't know anything about the modern

world. So why talk to them? But I was surprised. She related to me."

And so he went with it. Rolled the dice and saw what happened.

He was at the stage where your life lurches across crucial transitions, and she was past all that. He had to slow the velocity of his life to meet the velocity of hers. Thus an odd balance formed. It began at three afternoons a week. Another resident later hired Elvis to help with his physical therapy, a man crippled by a stroke, determined to walk again, and the home put him to work on weekends in the religious services department. Elvis found himself in the home nearly every day. He came so often, he knew most of the faces. Even other regular visitors—like one of the local TV weathermen, who made a regular pilgrimage to see an old professor—recognized him, nodded hello when they saw him in the corridor or the dayroom. Pretty much daily, he bounced in to see Ms. Oliver. He got paid for just three hours but saw her far more often. He wanted to. And so he became a fixture. Many intergenerational connections are fleeting, lacking density. Once in a while, though, youth and age in juxtaposition build into something luminous and eternal. Something having to do with two people liking each other, no matter their ages.

When he visited Ms. Oliver, he thought of his grandmother, Tete, back in the Dominican Republic, eighty and ailing with malignant tumors in her pancreas, stomach, and liver. When he was sixteen, he got a tattoo of Jesus on the underside of his right forearm, because he saw that as a way to remember her. Now he would look at Ms. Oliver and see Tete: "Her physical appearance for one. And her advice. And the way she speaks. Very clearly, very tranquil, very open-minded to new styles in the world. And we agree on a lot. Like we don't want any wars. 'Why should my child go to fight a war for someone else?' Those are her exact words."

They seemed a mismatched pair, for her life had very little to do with the future but with a current of memories, and his was all about the future, with events yet to happen. But they had a rapport, as if they had known each other in a previous incarnation, and a relationship that arose from the heart. They told each other everything, the entire spectrum of their inner lives, or just about, sometimes talking until their vocal cords were raw. Even though there was a full seventy-three years of separation, roughly three-quarters of a century, when they were together time collapsed. She made him feel older. He made her feel younger. As Ms. Oliver liked to say to him, "When we're together, it's like we're the same age."

She seldom left the home, didn't care that much to revisit the world beyond its doors, become once more absorbed in the bustling pace of the younger and more able. You had to be a different person to be out there is the way she saw it, and she wasn't that person anymore. Now and then, one of her daughters or an old friend would invite her out for a meal. They might say, "Wherever you want to go." She would insist on a place around the corner or down the block, anywhere in close proximity to the home, and to be honest she was perfectly happy if they just stayed in her room. The wheelchair, the hassle, it just scattered her mind. She had reconfigured her borders and was content. She felt safe here, and with her limited mobility and flawed sight, she didn't feel safe elsewhere. So her relationship with the young man was narrowly drawn in a physical sense. It was a relationship of conversation and imagination. In that respect, it was limitless.

Coming to the home and meeting Ms. Oliver was maybe the first positive experience for him that looked like it might endure. All his young life, he felt he had been cursed by bad luck, but perhaps this was it, the good luck that might balance some of the bad. He didn't know his future. But Ms. Oliver at least was pointing him to one.

"To go home, I have to pass through five different drug stops," he would always say. "Those are the opportunities I see. That's the success I see. The home shows me there's another future, another life. It keeps me out of the street, out of trouble, and teaches me how to be a professional. I don't have a profession yet, but I see that I can have one."

Ms. Oliver quickly came to understand his complicated life and its weight, and she helped him clarify his purpose, giving him impromptu lessons on life. Of course she needed him as much as he needed her. Elvis saw that right away.

"Every now and then I say, 'Why am I here?'" Ms. Oliver was saying to Elvis. "My answer is this is the way of life, and nature made it this way. So you deal with it as much as possible by distracting yourself. Otherwise you look around at the people who are worse than you, and you realize that could be you. Because you're not going to get better. You're not going to get younger. When you live in a nursing home, you lose anticipation. You're not anticipating meeting someone or going somewhere or seeing something new. That anticipation is a very big part of what's enjoyable about life. There isn't much to look forward to at this age."

Elvis piped up: "Miss Oliver, think of it as you're having a little vacation from everything you've done before."

"Oh, Elvis," she said. "You're like a breath of spring."

Ms. Oliver went on to say, "You know how to use a computer and all that, which is Greek to me. You can educate me on new things. The remote control. You're able to adjust it."

Elvis said, "It's a universal remote control. You have to program it."

"Okay, whatever that means."

"Don't worry, I'll program it for you."

"Thank goodness. Or else I'll have to hire an engineer or something."

He had to smile. Seeing her so much, he understood her alternative universe. "Reaching old age is loneliness, depression," is how he would explain it. "You don't feel you're part of the world anymore. You're in the way. You're a pest. You have to depend on someone. That disturbs Miss Oliver. My goal is to make her still feel part of the world."

In short order, he came to think of her as his oldest friend. He actually once told her straight out: "If I had never met you, I'd probably be dead or in jail. I grew up around drug dealers all my life. I wouldn't have any choice but to stand on the corner, too."

And so, in perhaps the most important hours of his week, he lost himself in the twisting labyrinth of this nursing home, and in particular, in Room 470, becoming true intimates with a wise old woman named Margaret Oliver who never thought of herself as a savior.

· *4* ·

Mozart was on the radio. Thursday. She closed her eyes, let herself drift. Ms. Oliver had her hands clasped across her chest, and she tapped her right foot to the music. A hairnet covered her hair. She kept it on a lot. As usual, she wore no makeup. She hadn't put on any since she came to the nursing home, didn't see any more point in prettifying her face. If there were ever a time to relax about your looks, take it from her, ninety-three had to be it. Accept her for what she was, was how she saw it, because that was all you were going to get.

So many uncontrollable factors when you are old. Wake up one day and you can't stand on brick-heavy legs. Wake up one day and you can't focus on anything, can't even see your own feet. Wake up one day and you can't remember yesterday. You have your good days, your bad days, and your oh-my-God days. Her arthritis today was raging. Bet on it; rain was coming.

She had been watching C-Span, where chattering heads were avidly discussing the different types of weapons used in war. It was too bleak to contemplate that, so she switched over to *Dr. Phil,* where the topic was runaway children. "Now when you saw that he wasn't there, did you miss him or were you relieved?" Dr. Phil was saying, in that laconic voice of his. Was that any better? She sighed. "There are not too many TV shows that I can lose myself in," she said to herself. On to Mozart.

Her possessions were few. She didn't need much anymore and had brought little to this new life. By now she had learned that when you're old, people take advantage of you and steal your stuff. She would save them the trouble by discarding it, no more of the clutter of the world. She owned just one piece of jewelry, an oblong ring with a blue stone that she always wore, a treasured gift from a grandchild. The room was pretty void of atmosphere. A gleam reflected off the polished linoleum floor. All her clothing was put away perfectly in the dresser against the wall, folded and piled up neatly, and in her narrow closet. Volunteers would accompany residents out to stores, Macy's and whatnot, take them there in a cab, but Ms. Oliver had no more interest in shopping; it was just so difficult getting around, and she had put in plenty of years of shopping, done her bit for consumer America. She was content to buy her clothes by mail order. A small television sat atop the dresser. Behind it was a bulletin board decorated with snapshots of her relatives and well-wishing cards and various certificates she had earned from the home for faithful attendance at its lecture courses. On the night table beside her bed was a scattering of large-print books she had borrowed from the home's first-floor library.

Taped to the wall, next to a sheet with the hours of the beauty parlor, was the cramped list of exercises that she was supposed to do each day for her arthritis.

1. Arm raises
2. Shoulder touch
3. Elbow at side, move arm right to left
4. Palms up, palms down
5. Bend wrist forward. Bend wrist back
6. Thumb to index finger. Thumb to middle finger. Thumb to ring finger. Thumb to pinky finger

Ms. Oliver had short steel-gray hair, plummy blue eyes. Her face was round, and her body was a little stouter than in her younger years. She was empathic and gregarious, with an inviting smile and lively laugh, easy to talk to. Her kindheartedness was well recognized. People were drawn to her. She was the kind of person hard to find anywhere. If you met her, you liked her. She was a specimen of tidiness, a former dressmaker, originally from Augusta, Georgia, who had married twice, her husbands long dead.

For her age, she was in enviable health. Ailments rarely
attacked her. Some years ago, she had had an operation for
back pain as well as a hysterectomy. Her blood pressure was
exemplary. A doctor once told her that he'd seen blood pressure like hers in a textbook but never in a human being,
and that pleased her, qualified her as a living medical curiosity. Physically, she was in decent shape, except for bad
osteoarthritis that made it difficult for her to walk or to grip
things with her hands. She would lament that her hands
were like butter; everything slid through them. She spent
almost all her time in a wheelchair, though she did some
walking each day in the hallway outside her room to try to
keep her joints oiled, a laborious undertaking that left her
spent. The arthritis was like a fierce undertow that kept her
from doing the things she was always able to do. She had a
touch of rhinitis, nasal congestion that caused her eyes to
tear. She always needed to have a tissue handy, to wipe away
the tears. And then there was her eyesight. She needed
bright light to distinguish between objects. It always seemed
too dark. Sometimes she would be clutching a balled-up tissue in her hand, and she couldn't tell it from the white
linoleum floor; everything just ran together. Was it in her
hand or wasn't it?

She still had a crackling good mind. No signs of dementia, just your occasional memory lapses. A sound mind in a
nursing home was good and bad. It was good, because whatever the shortcomings of her body, she could think and

process information and indulge in the bizarre twists of world events. For so many of the old these days, fear of losing your mind trumped fear of infirmities. No one wanted to be one of those Alzheimer's patients, a nonworking mind installed in a working body, a ruse of a person. So she was blessed. The bad part was that the home was crowded with the demented. She relished good conversation, and there was virtually no one stimulating to talk to.

Ms. Oliver's eyes were still closed when Elvis arrived. They exchanged the usual pleasantries, she gave him a seraphic smile, and he fetched her sweater. Her countenance began to change now that he was here. The very knowledge of his presence filled her with immense pleasure, wiped out the melancholy that sometimes crept into her days. Her speech was a little slurred. She had left her bridge downstairs to be fixed. A tooth had broken off. They went to the dayroom and found a choice spot.

The place was pretty full, doing good business as usual, and additional residents straggled in. Outside was a dark sky that wanted to rain. Some residents were able to hobble arthritically down from their rooms, but for many it was an odyssey just to get here. The dayroom was a chaos of women in wheelchairs, most of them inert, emaciated, cruelly smitten by the punishments of age, living out a past with an unchanging future—a frieze in barely detectable motion, and one had to wonder what was distracting God. Many sat mute or uttering clogged monosyllables, some attended by their frowning, glass-eyed companions. They seemed like married couples that had grown bored with each other. For them, one desultory day followed another. Dates on a calendar, whether the sun shone or the rain fell, whether wars raged or the stock market soared, these developments were background noise, if that. The rest of the world was just outside, but it seemed ten million miles away.

She said, "Elvis, do you drink orange juice?"

He said, "Yes, I do. It's my favorite drink."

"Well, that's good. You need it."

"You're going to be very proud of me. I ate very well for breakfast and took my vitamins."

"Very good. You really need to go exercise at the Y."

"Well, you know what I did? I went with my friend to the Y and played basketball. So what's new with you?"

"I haven't been doing too much. I'm worried about the war."

With all that was going on—terrorism, wars, companies shedding workers—Ms. Oliver often found her head spinning, unsure how to make sense of the world. Even with so little of her life in front of her, she was stubbornly interested in politics, the human shambles around the globe, for these were portentous times when everyone seemed consumed by the twists and turns of large events. One of the attractions to her of Elvis was that he, too, was deeply intrigued by politics. She and Elvis agreed that they didn't much care for President Bush, didn't much care for the invasion and troubled occupation of Iraq, oh what a sad president they had; both wondered how bleak the future was going to be. No matter her advanced age, Ms. Oliver remained a dutiful voter, sending her votes in by mail as absentee ballots, and she was a loyal Democrat.

She said, "I feel by attacking Iraq we're just antagonizing the terrorists more. I wish we could just warn Iraq and keep from doing anything. I've been so sad lately about everything that's happening. I lived through the Depression—we were lucky that my husband worked for the government—but we saw neighbors lose all their money. So the economy is bothering me and all the guns I hear about and the war. When I grew up, we didn't live with this. Kids, you know, didn't have guns."

Elvis said, "Yeah, well most people in my neighborhood have guns. I don't. But most people do. You run into somebody, and you have to wonder what he's got sitting there under his jacket. All I've got is a knife. And I have to tell you, that makes me a little vulnerable."

"Well, I don't want you to ever carry a gun; it's just trouble asking for more trouble. Elvis, tell me, do you know any young kids coming out of high school who are anxious to join the armed forces?"

"No, I don't."

"Because there are a lot of people who are doing it. I don't understand it. Is it an adventure thing or something else?"

"I think it's that they want to be men. I see these thirteen-fourteen-year-olds walking around with a cigarette in their hand. Because they want to be mature."

The trees outside were stained from an earlier rain. The dayroom was chilled. Ms. Oliver had on a blue dress. Around her neck was a thin chain, a key at her chest. It opened the drawer to her night table, the only thing she locked in her room. It was where she kept what little petty cash, bingo winnings and whatnot, that she had on hand.

They talked about his going to college. He wanted to learn physical therapy, seeing that as a reliable path to security and a regular life. After high school, he had needed some time off, to get a little money together and figure things out, but now he was going to enroll at the Brooklyn campus of Long Island University, taking courses part-time and still coming to the home. The president of the college had heard of his special relationship with Ms. Oliver and, impressed by his nature, offered him a full scholarship to the school to study in its physical therapy program.

Ms. Oliver said, "You're going to have to cut down your workload. Because you have to study, go to the library. School is a whole world unto itself."

"I'm ready. I know it's going to be hard. Nothing has come easy in my life."

"You have to know that getting a college education is very important. It will make a big difference in your life. I never was able to do it, but I made sure both my daughters did."

"It doesn't seem like you missed much not going to college. You're so smart."

"You miss something. I want you to see this through."

"Don't worry, I will. I don't give up on things."

The Jewish Home & Hospital had a good reputation. It was a sprawling tidy white brick building, actually several buildings united over the years, on Manhattan's Upper West Side, on West 106th Street, between Columbus and Amsterdam avenues. It stood on one of those numbered streets that also bore an honorific name, in this case Duke Ellington Boulevard. It was a wide street, a residential street, with a steady swish of traffic, food places squatting on the corners. The nursing home's transportation vans were usually parked outside. During the height of the terrorist alerts in the city, when people watched their backs, the "Jewish" name was painted over, so the home wouldn't be so inviting a target. The place was inhabited by a great range of residents, the majority of them trapped in some stage of dementia, the rich and the poor, the accomplished and the thwarted, all equalized by age and its heavy toll. Inside, it had an old-fashioned look. Certainly the place had its fill of immutable rules and not always accommodating aides, but there were rarely the persistent repugnant odors or the seedy bedragglement evident in the rooms of so many nursing homes. There was a pleasant garden on the first floor, bathed in shade trees, a goldfish pond, and barbecues. A nice library, a coffee shop. The home was plump with activities staged on a daily basis in the auditorium: Trivia Galore, Hebrew Club, Yiddish Club, College Course (this day's topic was Famous New Yorkers, Fiorello La Guardia), Game Night, Cabaret, Bingo, Music

Appreciation, Roseland Dance, Creative Writing, At the Movies, one activity after another, ways to move along the time.

"So you going to have a Chunky today?" Elvis asked Ms. Oliver. He watched her face with keen attention.

"What do you think?" she said. "I've got my bingo money. I've won three straight times." Her eyes blazed with joy.

"Boy, I wouldn't want to play against you, Miss Oliver."

The home's dog wandered by, and he wasn't much on looks. Elvis said, "That is the ugliest dog I have ever seen." His name was Elspeth, and one of the doctors had rescued him from a neglected home, holed up in a garage and not being fed. Now he lived at the nursing home, something for the residents to pet, and staff members took turns bringing him home for the weekend. The dog sniffed Ms. Oliver's shoes, and she said, "What are you doing there, huh?" and he moved on.

Elvis told Ms. Oliver that he was worried about a friend: "He's traveling around in the moon, as usual. He can't make up his mind on things."

Ms. Oliver said, "Remember what you learned from me about making decisions."

"Yes, learning how to say no."

"And then learning how to evaluate a situation and see if it changes. I've always been optimistic. Women talk about how they think when they reach forty that's a turning point. I always said I was having too much fun to notice I was forty. I've always followed a simple philosophy: Evaluate a situation, come to a logical solution, and proceed. Unless circumstances change, do that. Follow a way out, and that's it."

"Yeah, I told you how my brother had his first kid when he was fifteen. He has three kids, and he's twenty-six. With three different women. He didn't learn. Now he's learning. The difference between him and me is he just lives the moment. I look five years ahead. I got that from you."

"Well, I'm pleased to hear that."

"I've always been hard on myself. With schoolwork, I was hard on myself. With work, I was hard on myself. Because I had to prove something."

"You can't be too hard on yourself. The rest of the world is good enough at doing that."

"You know, I pretty much grew up with no mother or father. I became what a psychiatrist would call an obsessive compulsive person. Then I came here and met you, and I saw you laugh about things, and I calmed down. I take things easier because I see you do."

"That's a good way to be."

"I realize you can't satisfy everyone. It's not possible."

"No, it's not. To be able to get along with people is an art."

"It sure is an art."

His eyes stared fixedly into hers. "Miss Oliver, you make me feel I am someone," he said.

They continued feasting on the Chunky.

"Here's the last piece," he said.

"That's going to be my last Chunky," she said.

He arched his eyebrows: "Oh yeah, who you kidding?"

It would be night soon. A few more hours of activity. She would read some pages in her book. She would go to the bathroom, wash her face. She would go to bed, the day over.

· *5* ·

Old people. Why do the young patronize them? Why do they make them invisible, irrelevant? Ms. Oliver wondered these things. Maybe these were indulgent thoughts, furtive objections that billowed out when she heard one too many patronizing "Dearies" or "Sweeties" or saw yet another cross look when she asked for help to do something she could no longer do. Sitting in the dayroom, she told Elvis: "My son-in-law said that Eskimos used to put the old people up with the walruses, which ate them, and then they killed the walruses. There's a tribe in Africa, I heard, where after a certain age they put old people up in the hills and let them fend for themselves. In the East Indies, I read, it used to be the case that if the husband died, the wife would have to die too. They would cremate the man, and she would have to burn up with him. She would have to be buried with him."

Elvis rolled this information over in his mind, walruses gnawing away at old people, their wasting away up in the mountains, shooing away danger with weak limbs—what was this! Too much to digest, too hard to fathom.

"America is between neutral and disrespectful to the old," she said. "It looks good compared to having the walruses eat them, but they don't respect them nearly enough. They hide them and ignore them. Out of sight, out of mind."

Elvis frowned. His perspective having been shaped by this woman, he came at it in a different way. Old people, why, they were a national treasure. "We ought to look up to old people, not dis them," he said. "They know so much. Look at you. I can't believe all you know. You're like a dictionary or an encyclopedia. You know, like, everything."

She beamed at him. That Elvis, what a charmer. She once suggested he go into the ministry; boy, would he be perfect.

This was a Wednesday, as it happened. It was a summer afternoon. The room was drenched with wavering white light.

Then: "You know, Elvis, I don't hate old age. When you realize what the world is and you realize you're a great-grandmother and you see some young man get told the war is over in Iraq and he gets shot to death guarding a bank—that young man never had a chance—how can I hate old age? I think to myself, I've lived all these years. This is how it is. I feel frustrated for myself. I feel angry at what I can't do. But I don't feel sorry for myself. I refuse to feel sorry for myself."

"That makes a lot of sense," Elvis said. "Everyone has to get old, unless they get shot or run over, so it's not like anyone's picking on you by making you old."

"It's like makeup. I don't see any reason to put on makeup or lipstick. Until I came here, I put on makeup. I've never done it since I came here. I accept that I'm old. Why hide what nature has done to me? I accept it. And I don't wear jewelry. Some of the others get their nails done and put on all sorts of cosmetics. Nature has done things to me I can't control. Nature has made me an old woman. I don't see any point in decorating myself. On television, I see all these girls talking about makeovers, makeovers. Why? There's nothing ever said about their brains or their personalities—it's the look."

"Yeah, I hear you. It's this consumer society. Spend the money and make yourself young. Make yourself look like somebody else, but inside you're still you; there're no operations for that."

"You know, Elvis, life is something like a good book. A long time ago, I read a book, and it was such a good book that I didn't want to finish it. I put off reading the last two or three pages for days. Then I finished it, and it was over. Life is like that. It has an end. At some point it's all over, and there's nothing you can do about it. A man here told me that he liked peanut butter so much that when his mother gave him a sandwich he would go down by the river and hold it and hold it. He didn't want to eat it. Then he ate it. It was like me and the book."

"Well, if your life is a book, it's a really good one, one of the best, I can tell you that much," Elvis said.

She smiled at him. Most of the time, they meshed so well together, he saying just the right thing. Now and then, unprompted, she would want to talk about being old, and he would grow quiet and listen. She said, "I never thought about growing old. It just slipped up on me. How many years I was never bothered me. Once I became old, I was surprised. Nobody told me what it was like to be old. It just creeps up on you. I started falling from time to time. And not being able to do things for myself. When your mind works, as mine does, you see most of the deficiencies. I was always so independent. I hate being dependent on the aides. I didn't feel when you got old you'd be so dependent. I thought when you got old you'd look different and not run around as much. I didn't know there would be all the aches and pains. I didn't know I'd get the arthritis. I remember when I was young I had an aunt who was always complaining about her arthritis, and I'd think, I wish she'd stop complaining about it. I mean, it was so annoying. Now I know."

"Well, you've got a really good attitude. I like that about you."

"Well, I push back in my mind that my life is ending. And I know that it is. After all, young children are killed and born with deformities and get illnesses, and here I am ninety-three. I've seen a lot of death. I saw so many people die from the first flu epidemic when I was eight or nine. Whole families were dying. There was nothing to treat it. I've seen a lot of wars. Death happens. I was never a worrier. Some people are worrywarts. I just did what I had to do. I just don't want to have pain. I want to go fast and not suffer. I'm not unhappy. I would be unhappy without you coming to see me."

"Well, that's nice of you to say. I like coming and seeing you more than anything."

"Elvis, I was talking to a couple of the aides. One said her grandmother lived to 111. Another one said her grandmother lived to 113. Can you imagine?"

"Wow, that is something. We have some people here who are over a hundred."

There had been a few feature stories about centenarians, the fastest-growing age bracket in the country, demographers speculating that by 2050 there might be a million people in triple digits. All of us, living interminable golden years, starring in a play going on a little too long, whether we wanted to or not.

Elvis said he had heard that the oldest person in New York had died in a nursing home upstate, a woman who was

110 and was thought to be the eleventh oldest person in the country, four years younger than the oldest. She was a rabid baseball fan, and on her 110th birthday, she sang "Take Me Out to the Ball Game."

Ms. Oliver said, "Nobody teaches us about aging. But I decided myself to come to a nursing home. I couldn't subject my kids to what I needed. This is really the best place for me."

"Yeah, I can see that. You feel you made the right decision?"

"Yes, I do, I really do, and I've thought about it."

"You feel you regret it?"

"No. See, Elvis, they have entertainment here. A lot of old people, they live with their family, and they're in their room all day staring at four walls. Their family is coming and going, and they just sit there like a useless lump. They need something, and who's going to get it? Here you ring the bell, and someone comes."

"Yeah, you get lonely otherwise. I understand that."

"You know, I've never been a depressed person. I've had episodes. There were times here when I felt like falling down and crying. Like if I haven't heard from the girls for a few days, that can set me off. Why aren't they here to do something for me? If I'm in the dining room and I hear the women groaning—ahhahahah—and muttering, I'll think, Why am I here?—there's no escape. I look at the other residents as just strangers. I can't have a conversation with them. I don't resent them. If you're in a foreign land, you try to speak to what extent you can to them, but you're not really part of that world. That's how I look at things here. I'm not really part of this world. So I'll come into my room and put on some music or talk to someone on the phone or wait for you to arrive, and it all changes."

"Yeah, I see what you're trying to say; you sort of make your own world. I do that too when I see the things happening on the streets in my neighborhood. I go into my room and write some music and forget what's out there."

"One thing I've decided is if I'm here I want to be free of all responsibility. I used to have this calendar on which I had people's birthdays and who I had to call and what I had to do. No more. I don't need the pressure. When you're old, you don't have to worry about love affairs and money. You don't have to worry about your future. You know what it is. You don't have to plan your week or your next day. I must say, that's very liberating."

She appreciated that there was plenty he knew that she didn't, that she could learn things from him. Once she asked him whether he was into rap music, a total enigma to her, and he said, sure, he liked to rhyme with his friends, do some battles. He told her about his notebooks filled with lyrics. She learned about CDs from him.

She wagged her head: "I'm still puzzled how they get messages up to outer space."

"Satellites, Miss Oliver," Elvis said. "I was watching this

movie the other night, *Behind Enemy Lines*. Robert Redford was in enemy territory. Our intelligence was able to find out where he was by satellite."

"You know, Elvis, when I was a little girl we used to sit on the stoop and look up at the moon and wonder, Wouldn't it be something if a person could get up on the moon?—never thinking I'd live to see men land on the moon. And now it seems so long ago that they did it."

"It has been a while."

"Well, with all these inventions, it amazes me they can't do anything about the aging brain," she said, weakly straightening her shoulders.

Elvis frowned at that. "Yeah, that's something they ought to be working on," he said. "Though I know a lot of younger brains that could use some working on. Your brain works better than most of the ones I know."

Some commotion at the entrance. A resident was being wheeled out on a stretcher, rumbling along the sidewalk, and loaded carefully into an ambulance. No telling about the gravity. He might return, or not. This was part of the backdrop.

She asked Elvis, "Do you go to rap concerts?"

"No, I don't go to any of that. I like some of the music. Certain movements. We call it flows."

"Well, Elvis, don't you go dancing to the discotheques."

"I don't go anywhere. Basically, me and my friends come

to my house, and we may have a few drinks and listen to music and rhyme. And that's till twelve. Then everyone has to leave, and I go to bed. And that's only on the weekend.

"And there's no smoking in my room. Friends call me Bloomberg"—after the New York mayor, who virtually banished smoking in the city.

She liked that part, putting down a health edict.

"You know I've always been psychic," she said. "My kids used to say I was a witch. They'd say, 'Mother, you're a witch; how did you predict that?' My son-in-law's a psychologist, and he says that doesn't happen, but I wonder."

"I think I believe in that."

"Did I tell you about the day my first husband died?"

"No, I don't think so."

"That day I came home from work a little late, because I stopped to buy some special cookies that the family wanted. We had a very pleasant evening. No one fought with anybody. But you know how something sometimes keeps flashing through your head? Death flashed through my head over and over. Death, death, death. I was tired and went to bed before my husband. He wanted to sit up a bit longer and listen to the radio. He was in his easy chair. I turned down the radio a bit so I could sleep and went to bed. All that night, death kept staying with me in my sleep. Death, death, death. The next morning, I woke up and I just knew. He wasn't in the bed beside me. I went into the other room, and he was still there in the easy chair. He died in his sleep, just like that. And I knew it was going to happen."

"Boy, that's some story," Elvis said. "I don't think you're a witch, but I do think you're psychic or something."

"I think so, too, but maybe it's best if we keep it to ourselves."

"Okay, let's do that. That makes sense. We don't want to scare anybody."

"Yes, and I feel that there's some kind of mental telepathy between us."

They had gotten so close that they felt they were plugged into each other's mind. Whenever Ms. Oliver needed help with something, Elvis seemed to materialize. The other day, she wanted the tape flipped in her tape player, and her arthritic hands couldn't manage it. Sorcererlike, Elvis appeared.

Aides sometimes hectored them about all the time they spent together: "What are you two, an 'item'?" Ms. Oliver would laugh and say, "I'm almost seventy-five years older than Elvis. Some item!"

She looked at the clock, giving an exaggerated sigh, the desultory day nearing its conclusion.

The dinner hour. He took her upstairs. She ate in the common dining area in the middle of her floor, a grouping of tables for four, a big-screen TV in the corner, the news on, a hit-and-run getting the full action-news treatment. The tables seated two on one side, two on the other, just enough space to squeeze in a meal on a tray. On the wall beside her was a board that gave the day, the date, the next holiday, the season, the weather—the latest particulars at a timeless place.

When you went to dinner, what a commotion. There was often a litany of complaint. You quickly understood everybody's etiology.

"What are you yapping about?"

"My thunder thighs, what do you think?"

"They're awful. Scrap 'em. Kill 'em."

"You're looking ugly today."

"Why, thank you."

There were no trajectories there that she wanted to follow.

Elvis slid her into her assigned spot, same place breakfast, lunch, and dinner, beside demented women she could not talk to. That's the way the cycle of life went in this building. She habitually ate in fifteen minutes. ("I get out of that dining room so quickly. I fly out of there back to my room.") Why dither? The behavior of the other residents just got her petulant. She always told one woman she must have gone to Boss College, because all she did was boss everybody around.

Once, telling Elvis about how inane so much of the dinner conversation was, how she coped with it by paying complete attention to her food, she said she occasionally felt like standing up and shouting, "So what did you think of the president's latest speech?" But she hadn't yet mustered the courage to do it, not that she expected anything in response but blank stares.

She had composed a poem about one of the men in the dining room, always up and lamenting some indiscretion.

Sit down, Mr. Brown
Turn around
It's time to dine.
If you don't frown
You'll get a glass of wine.

The woman who sat nearest her, deep into dementia, sometimes cursed a blue streak, an apparent rebellion at her diminished state. Every day she played the upright piano in the hallway, always the same song.

At meals, she incessantly picked on Ms. Oliver. She would say, "You're always dropping things on the floor." Ms. Oliver would respond, "I'm not dropping anything." But there was no dissuading her. "You are dropping something," she would insist. So Ms. Oliver would say, "Well, if I don't drop things, what will the cleaners pick up?" Or when Ms. Oliver laid her napkin down on the table once she had finished, the woman would bark, "Don't throw that my way. Keep it away from me." Ms. Oliver would shoot her a sour glance and say, "Shut right up."

Or, referring to her wheelchair, the obstreperous woman would say, "Don't touch my machine. If you break it, you'll pay for it." The other day, when she rolled in, the woman said, "All these big-ass people."

Her ululations the night before hit Ms. Oliver like stones. "I feel like I'm part of a street gang," she said.

"You can't let it bother you," Elvis said. "She can't help it. You have to be open-minded and just ignore her."

Well, here was Elvis giving her words of wisdom.

Twenty years talking to ninety-three. She had to admit: twenty years was right. She cooled off.

The telltale sound of the big silver cart loaded with the trays of food rumbling down the hall. Aides were available to fetch the dinners, but Elvis liked to handle hers when he was around. When the cart slid to a stop alongside the tables, Elvis waved off assistance and retrieved her meal, everything arranged in a triangle formation on the apple-green platter. He plonked it down in front of her and draped around her neck one of those nearly full-body napkins, the kind the servers give you at seafood restaurants when you order lobster. He grabbed some straws for her beverages: one for her soup, one for her tea, one for her cranberry juice, and one for her milk. A four-straw dinner.

Now that she was all set and had sampled her first mouthful, not much consternation from the other tables, Elvis bent over and gave her a gentle peck on the cheek. He told her good-bye, all his normal civilities, the day folding itself up around him. He went downstairs, past some lingerers in the dayroom, past the security guard handing someone a pass. He moved through the automatic doors, and they whooshed shut behind him.

· *6* ·

Want to buy something? That was the message, the natter-
ing nonstop message. When you came out of the subway at
Saint Nicholas Avenue and 181st Street, in Washington
Heights, the upper tip of Manhattan, riding up a voluminous, lurching elevator to reach the street, you were greeted
with a commercial explosion, goods-glutted merchants
cramped one on top of each other, the streets bursting with
people hawking wares. Lucille Roberts Fitness for Women.
Raquel Ninos. New York Sneakers. Loco-Loco. Blooming
Sol. Daysi Travel. Real Deals. The bargains hammered away
at you whichever direction you walked. The advertisements
a run-on blur, incantatory. Everything emblazoned with
come-ons, dollar signs: two for $5, three for $8, two pairs
of baby sneakers for $5, shirts for $2.99, $3.99, $1.99, 50

percent off. Buy shoes. Buy fruit. Buy shirts. Buy a vacation. Buy a couch. Buy dope. Racks of clothes spraddled on the sidewalk, fruit on the sidewalk, shoes on the sidewalk. A man had a rickety workbench set up, a table saw humming on it, and he did repairs for people right there—fix your toaster, build some shelves, out here in the open, low overhead.

You could even buy divorce, get yourself a new start. A travel agency brazenly advertised in its window: "Divorce. $199. Easy. Legal. Fast. No Need to Go to Court. Spouse Signature Not Required."

Buy. Buy. Buy.

It was all so ironic in this too-often troubled, sad-sack neighborhood, teeming with drug dealers and ghosts and busted dreams, walls an explosion of graffiti, people scraping by but always being implored to pull out any idle money and buy.

Drug dealers had considerable hegemony on the streets and alleyways and building hallways. Everyone knew who they were, where to find them, what they had for sale. In the mid-1980s, Washington Heights distinguished itself as the outright capital of crack cocaine. Influxes of Dominican immigrants transformed the area into the largest wholesale drug market, all the bridges and highways that converged on the neighborhood making it an easy trip from suburban America, as well as the rest of the city. In the early 1990s, when the neighborhood hit its nadir, drug arrests averaged one every hour and a half, and the cops still never got everybody. Killings transpired at such a frenzied clip that at funeral homes occupied coffins stood in the halls because all the private viewing rooms were taken. (You were dead, and you still had to wait in line.) Now, after a pronounced police push, crime was a lot less than it had been a decade ago, real estate values had become buoyant, but pockets of the area remained insistently unsettling. Crack had gravitated to other neighborhoods, and the drugs proffered on the streets of Washington Heights were marijuana, ecstasy, and zip syrup.

The neighborhood ran from 145th Street to 200th Street, sliced by Broadway, what some knew as "Dominican Avenue." In the blink of an eye, the tone of the street could change from calm to menace. Sometimes, in the night, you could smell the stink of fear in the air. A wanted poster, which decorated the windows of some of the shops, announced a ten-thousand-dollar reward for information on the whereabouts of a man accused of stabbing a livery driver in the neck and robbing him. Crime was still an integral part of the neighborhood's atmosphere. If there was a distinctive enough angle to it, it made the paper. Today's dailies gave good play to a shooting: Four people, two of them Head Start teachers, were shot when a man began firing his gun on Saint Nicholas between 186th and 187th streets. The teachers were going into the Four Star Dollar Store. The other two were standing in front of the Remesas Quis Que Yana store. A man drove up, pointed a gun out the window, and pulled the trigger. One of the men shot was apparently the target; the others happened to get in the way—a common way to die here. This crime occurred in the afternoon. People in the neighborhood don't feel they need to settle their grudges inside or under cloak of darkness; they do it whenever they feel like doing it. In one respect, the story was somewhat unusual. None of the four died. They had a lucky day in Washington Heights.

"What up?" Elvis asked.

"Nothin', man," his friend said. "What up with you?"

"Not much," Elvis said. "Chillin'. You working?"

"Yeah, over at the rec center. You?"

"Yeah, I'm working."

"Still at that home?"

"Yeah, still at the home."

Back when he started, his friends couldn't figure it out. Why was he spending all his free time at an old folks home, with doddering people four and five times his age, some of them not even able to name the president or the year or to add one and one and get something? Why was he there, day after day, hardly being paid a cent for sitting with them and wheeling them to the bathroom and bingo? Was he going through some goody-goody phase? He would try to explain, but they wouldn't get it. He would try to tell them that some of the old people in the home were more alive than they were. They had accomplished a life worth living. He was learning primal things, and he was doing something meaningful in a world that, senseless as it might seem, made a lot more sense than his crazed world. He felt sure this work was going to lead to something, help him turn his life around. He just had to give it time.

His friends relaxed their ribbing the day he told them he had begun to get paid by the home and some of the residents. They understood doing just about anything if there was cash involved, even though that wasn't his motivation.

He was standing outside A. J. Fashions, his favorite clothing store, practically his only clothing store. It was busy, the aisles packed, teenagers entering and leaving, looking for fly clothing. It was near the barbershop where his brother cut hair. Pretty much everything in his closet originated from A. J. Fashions. Elvis was a careful dresser. He dressed in the hood look, the urban hip-hop look. Everything baggy. Clothes were a challenge on his skimpy income, but he boasted strong negotiating skills. "See this Hucker shirt," he said once. "It costs an arm and a leg. I got it for a finger. Because I hustle for it. I bargain. I can get something down to half price some days." Since the employees at A. J. Fashions knew he spent so much there, they listened to his arguments, how he had enough to pay half the price, but nothing more, and sometimes they gave in and sometimes they didn't.

The summer sun blazed down, baking the gaggle of pedestrians, auguring a long hot evening. It was so hot, it made you blurry in your thinking. It was hard to focus on someone walking by and remember to say "What up?" to someone you knew really well. You could hear the window air conditioners groaning, working nonstop to keep up with the heat.

A couple of women in housedresses sat at the edge of the sidewalk in metal folding chairs, talking, gesturing, pumping gossip into the air, while kids bunched outside the apartment buildings and on the street corners, yukking it up, just lurking, staring, watching afternoon slide to twilight and beyond. Rats impudently sniffed garbage, looking for something worthwhile, gravitating from trash pile to trash pile. Cars drifted down the avenue, American, years old, with mangled fenders and mufflers overdue for a stop at Midas. Their radios blasted rap music.

Elvis stood with his hands interlaced in front of him. He knew a lot of people in the neighborhood. His world was these streets and the home, almost no place else, and he would say "Hey" and "What up?" to a hundred people a day here, mostly kids a little chewed up, knowing a harder life than in most neighborhoods.

His friend, his stubbled face trained on the pedestrian traffic, gave the eye to two barely teenage girls, their mouths full of braces, in shorts that must have been sewn on, preposterously high heels, swinging their behinds as they passed. They had okay faces.

"Check it out," he said, barely containing his lust.

"I'm checking it," Elvis said. His eyes turned to the side-walk, and he followed them down.

"They're asking for it," his friend said. He shook his head.

Girls and women in the neighborhood, he realized, were known to be loose with men and to set traps for them beneath the sheets to get them to marry them. Except few men did.

You could hear distant sirens. A bottled water delivery truck buzzed past, honking its horn.

"Those girls need to get a brain," Elvis murmured. He kept his gaze steady, betraying no particular interest or excitement.

His friend raised an eyebrow.

Elvis was dismissive of girls who strutted around in suggestive clothing, tiny wisps of dresses or tight shorts, and the most expensive frilly underwear they could afford, their sole goal at their young age being to stimulate the interest of boys. He saw that as perpetuating the ghetto cycle: boys, babies, truancy, poverty, drugs, prison, death.

He looked down at the ground, scuffed the toe of his sneaker on the sidewalk.

"That girl has some behind," his friend said. She could have been fourteen or twenty-two. You couldn't tell for sure.

"Yeah" was all Elvis managed to say.

Some friends passed by, paused to give Elvis a pound, the urban handshake, bump shoulders. They said they were going downtown to mess around, see you.

He moved through the street like a bubble, so much to see, so much best not to see, memories scratched into every corner. An old guy walked up to his car, yanked a parking ticket off the windshield, tore it in half, and tossed it on the pavement. Elvis was supposed to smile, and so he did.

Then the barbershop where Ronny cut hair. Elvis said hello to his brother and dropped into a chair, leafed through a magazine. He didn't need a haircut, just killing time. Ronny looked clean and neat in jeans and T-shirt. Mirrors everywhere, hair on the floor. The place was thronged with teenagers, their interminable chatter reverberating through the shop. One older man was waiting, sucking on a toothpick in his mouth, scowling at a newspaper. Ronny supplied some commentary—business going well, yeah, the girlfriend's okay, saw Mom the other day—as he worked on the hair.

Elvis scooped up a copy of *Sucesos*, a favorite among Dominicans, which devoted much of its contents to how people died in the Dominican Republic. The deaths were always repugnant ones, stuff you didn't want to imagine. A guy sliced up a girl. Someone had his head chopped off. Ronny read this magazine all the time, derived something from the misery. Elvis sometimes leafed through it when he was in the barbershop or saw it lying around somewhere. "But I don't like it," he said. "It brings me back. I've seen enough of that death. There are times my brother sees someone he knows in there. It's creepy."

The cover story was about the devil causing fires in a town. Then there was a piece about a baby being poisoned. Every other page featured another gruesome death. And there was always a picture of a naked woman tucked near the back of the slender magazine, usually frisking in the ocean, the water lapping at her thighs, an unexpected interruption in the blood flow.

He picked up another issue, this one with a cover scoop about a diabetic cat with long claws killing a woman, a bloodied picture of the victim, a scary photo of the cat, looking like it could take just about anyone. Enough.

Done with the street, Elvis climbed the stairs to his apartment and languidly tidied up his room, wanting it to look better than the rest of the place. He herded some clothing into the closet, put away a pair of shoes. No one else was home, and that was good news. He settled in to work on some rhymes that he wrote down in composition books. He had a stack of them in his dresser, pages and pages of rhymes.

He lived in a building just off Saint Nicholas Avenue, a funereal structure above a dry cleaner and next to a library. He rented a dust-speckled room inside a cramped two-bedroom apartment. He had always lived in rooms. This was the fourth place he had called home since leaving his brother. None of them had been anything that felt like his.

The apartment belonged to a woman who spent much of her time in the Dominican Republic. She was in her sixties and didn't seem to do much of anything beyond drinking, which she did well. She liked to hang out at a nearby grocery store, where she drank her beer and her Johnnie Walker. She had a deep and appreciative kinship with Johnnie Walker. Elvis had little use for her. She wasn't someone you could ever have a coherent conversation with, because she was always potted. She was so scrawny, you could see her blood vessels. He hardly ever saw her eat much. She might boil a couple of eggs, and that would be it. She would wash the eggs down with Johnnie Walker.

Elvis had known her since he was ten. She was one of those neighborhood characters that everyone knew. Whenever there was a parade or street fair or something, she would strut out to the middle of the street, inebriated, and start dancing with abandon. When Elvis was working in his mother's food truck, he would often see her making a drunken spectacle of herself, in some world no one else could quite fathom. She told him once that she had been married to a famous Dominican musician and had had a son with him, but Elvis didn't buy the story. "I don't see how she could have been married and had a kid. She's a drunk."

To meet the rent, and turn some profit on top of it, she rented out the apartment to as many people as she could shoehorn into it. There was a cramped living room with a couple of shabby couches and a cot, two tiny bedrooms, a bathroom, and an angular kitchen with ancient appliances and a small dinette table, all of it usually suffused in a gray darkness.

When Elvis first moved in, a guy was living there alone in the sepulchral murk. He was a drug dealer. One day, he took a brick of cocaine from his drug source on consignment. He never paid for it. The source came around looking for him, intending to kill him, but he had disappeared. The source was still looking for him.

Until recently, Elvis shared the place with four other people. When the woman was around, she would sleep on one of the couches in the living room. Elvis had one of the bedrooms, which cost him a hundred dollars a week, payable in cash. A guy who was a friend of the woman's rented the cot in the living room. A woman in her midtwenties had the other bedroom.

Elvis referred to the guy who slept on the cot as the Dope Fiend. He was always jacked up on drugs. He would snort cocaine and inject heroin, a combination called bread with butter. He was constantly making Elvis late for work, because he would be in the bathroom doing dope when Elvis needed to shower and get ready to leave. One morning, Elvis discovered him passed out in the bathroom. This was during the winter, and he was lying with his head against the radiator. Elvis pulled him off it, and the man's right temple was burned. He couldn't wake him up, so he left him on the floor and took his shower. One time, the Dope Fiend put the moves on the young woman, and, emphatically uninterested, she threatened to kill him if he tried that again.

A few months before, the Dope Fiend had finally moved out. Elvis had no idea where he went, but he was elated that he was gone.

The young woman was separated from her husband, who was a drug dealer, the neighborhood's seeming occupation of choice. They had a two-year-old daughter who sometimes stayed with the mother and sometimes stayed with the father. The woman had a girlfriend she was romantically involved with who lived with her in her room. Elvis called the lot of them "a dysfunctional family and a half." He couldn't stand his roommates. For one thing, the women kept the apartment a mess. There was a bucket in the bathroom for garbage, and yet Elvis would go in and it would be empty and the floor would be littered with their refuse, including their used Kotex. He couldn't believe it. Weren't they embarrassed to be dropping their Kotex on the floor? Elvis used the bathroom as little as possible. The kitchen was nearly as repulsive. The women would leave food in the refrigerator until it spoiled. Once, looking for a snack, he opened it and found a turkey that must have been there for about a decade. He just about passed out from the stench. Even now, long after it had been disposed of, there was still a whiff of that turkey every time you yanked open the wheezing refrigerator. And the sink. They left dirty dishes piled up in it for days. Often the drain was clogged, and the dishes would be sitting there submerged in filthy water. It finally got so bad a plumber had to come and work a snake through the drain, and rice and spoiled meat came pouring out. Elvis couldn't bear the thought of trying to cook a meal in that kitchen, and so he didn't. He ate his lunch at the home, and he would either eat his dinner at a local hangout or pick up a sandwich to have in his room.

He had no idea what the two women did for a living. They would lounge around the apartment all day and venture out in the evening. They told him they worked at a restaurant. He figured they were probably strippers or maybe prostitutes. They'd return around four in the morning, drunk, fumbling to try to fit the key in the lock, and more often than not Elvis would have to get up and let them in.

Soon after the Dope Fiend left, the women moved out, too. Elvis didn't know why or where they went, but he wasn't complaining, that was for sure.

A new man had just assumed their room, and he seemed just fine. He was a war veteran, in his fifties, who had a regular job he went to at four in the morning, something in delivery. He was the opposite of the women, extremely neat. He kept the bathroom nice, the kitchen clean. He wasn't drunk all the time. Elvis could actually talk to the man, and he would say something comprehensible back.

Elvis's room was a plain room, a lonely room, a sad room. It never felt like a place to live in, just a space to sleep. It was maybe ten by fifteen feet, entered by two French doors. The floor was black-and-white linoleum tiles, more than a few of them splintered. It was a furnished room, but the furnishings were as defeated as the neighborhood. There was a lumpy double bed, a peeling dresser with an oval mirror, a wobbly nightstand with a small television and a game player, and three mismatched chairs, a stark absence of color. The apartment was on the second floor, easily reachable from the street, and yet he couldn't lock any of his windows. The windows barely stayed in the dinged-up frame. He would push one up, and it would fall out of the frame; if he didn't grab it, he would have no window at all.

He kept a can of Raid on the windowsill. It was the most important object in the room. The apartment, a victim of slatternly housekeeping, was thick with roaches. The landlord wasn't about to pay for an exterminator, and none of the tenants could afford the cost. So everyone cohabitated with roaches. Elvis kept his bed pulled a few inches from the wall, hoping that would prevent roaches from crawling on him as he slept. When his friends visited, he cautioned them to check the seat of the chair before they sat down. Dressing in the morning, he always shook out his clothes, so he wouldn't end up wearing roaches to work. When he would sit on his bed at night reading or watching television, he always was looking for bugs out of the corner of his eye; if he spied one, he would bound up, grab the Raid, and fire. On some nasty nights, forty or fifty of them would get wiped out in one brutal massacre.

"Look at this; we have a visitor," Elvis said, narrating this intrusion for a friend. A roach was inching its way down the wall. "This is what I do all day." He scooped up the Raid can and squirted the roach once, twice, three times. He watched it, made sure it perished. "They're warriors," he said. "You have to shoot them about five times. This is my life. I'll be reading a book and have to get up and shoot roaches."

One roach down. A second appeared, taking its chances. Elvis fired. Two down.

"Man, these bugs, I don't believe them today. They're courageous."

A third roach wandered along the windowsill. It caught Elvis's eye. "Man, I need reinforcements," he moaned. "They won't quit. Call in the reserves."

He squirted. Three down.

"Yeah, three down," he said. "Maybe three hundred to go."

If he had learned anything in this relentless bug war, it was that he had no hope of victory. Containment was the best he could expect, and even that was a struggle, the odds running against him.

Things that really mattered to him he kept on the dresser. There was a picture frame containing three snapshots, the faces of his brother's three kids by three mothers: Anthony, nine, Melody, seven, and Destiny, two. His brother was currently living with another woman. At the moment, Anthony was in the Dominican Republic, so Elvis didn't see him, but the other two he saw. They were with their mothers in the neighborhood.

A two-dollar bill was stuck in the mirror. He got it from an anonymous donor. When he was in high school, he received a two-thousand-dollar scholarship from the city's Department for the Aging for his intergenerational work. An anonymous donor matched it and sent him a two-dollar bill to boot. He was proud of that two dollars.

He had a thirst. He sauntered into the matchbox kitchen, the afterscent of past meals lingering in the air, and got himself a drink of water in a flyspecked glass and ravenously drank it down. He flopped on the bed, rain now bucketing down outside, the poorly set windows rattling in their moorings. He clicked on the TV and watched cartoons, the way he liked to finish the day. His favorite was the Japanese cartoon *Dragon Ball Z*. It revolved around a group of scornful warlords who tirelessly hunted for seven mystical orbs that afforded command of the cosmos. A troop of courageous martial arts heroes led by Goku stood in the way.

Caught up in cartoons, the animated stunts and

adventures, was how he and his brother used to conclude their uneventful days when they lived together with their mother, sleeping on separate sandwich beds in the living room, escaping to an imaginary world that had to be better than their real one.

· 7 ·

Today Elvis and Ms. Oliver clucked about Birthday Girl. It was their code name for one of the aides, let them camouflage their gossip, who'd said what, who'd done what. They had pseudonyms for several of their favorite conversational subjects.

Ms. Oliver was always wary of what she said; you couldn't be too careful. Both she and Elvis agreed: "These walls have ears." The home was full of recognizable and unrecognizable people coming and going, and many of them had a nosy interest in what the residents talked about. Ms. Oliver and Elvis shared a fondness for gossip about the home, but they would rather have the workers excavate information on their own than get it by eavesdropping on private conversations.

Thus the code names. Birthday Girl earned hers because

she repeatedly told residents it was her birthday; weren't they going to get her something nice? Shamelessly drumming up gifts. Did that they didn't know how many times. The Big Bad Wolf was another story, a particularly surly and intimidating aide. You had to watch what you said to her, so stinging was her wrath. There was the Puppet, the appellation earned because she allowed herself to remain under the influence of the Big Bad Wolf. Then the Blue Cock. No matter what, he was always right. Others looked up to him, deferred to his judgment. He was the Blue Cock with his hens. But he was good-hearted.

Ms. Oliver said, "That Big Bad Wolf, she reminds me of a poem I know of a little girl who had a curl that hung down her forehead. When she was good, she was very, very good, and when she was bad, she was horrid."

Elvis said, "I like that; I'll have to write that down."

"You know what the Big Bad Wolf used to say when you first came here? That you were fresh."

"Yeah, fresh. A man would be falling on the floor, and they would be talking about Avon and I cooked this with that. I'd say, 'Do something!' I guess that's being fresh."

Ms. Oliver didn't argue with what he said.

"I go home and I dwell on these things, and I'm punching my bed. Because you guys are so vulnerable here. The aides say, well, they have problems. I've had problems, too."

Ms. Oliver said, "Oh, I have another name I gave to someone."

"What's that?"

"The Bear."

"The Bear? Who could that be?"

"Think about it. A bear is someone who hugs you to death."

Elvis gave that some thought. "Oh, that aide who you were ringing and she wouldn't come and you got impatient?"

"That's right. She was very nice. But she has a short temper. She was mad at me for ringing the bell. She was so ignorant, and then when she realized she was wrong, she was so nice to me, flattering me every which way, going on and on and on. So I call her the Bear. She'll hug you to death."

"That's perfect."

"So let's add the Bear to our list of names."

"Consider it done."

"The Bear is not a young person, and I feel that sometimes she finds this gets too much for her. It's not that she's a mean person. She can't take it."

"Well, if you can't take it, you should try something else. It's selfish when you can't keep your temper. I don't believe in that."

Ms. Oliver mentioned that she fell today, nothing serious, a small slip.

"I came in once, and you were on the floor."

"Yes, I felt myself slipping, and I just sat down. So it wasn't a real fall in any sense."

"Yeah, it's like you sat down when you weren't intending to sit down."

"I have these silly impulses sometimes. Once I was sitting in my chair and my dress was twisted, and I said to myself, 'The next person who comes by I'm going to stand up and have them pull my dress down.' So this man came by, and I asked him. He pulled it down, and I said to him, 'I suppose you never pulled one down, but I'll bet you pulled plenty up.' I was thinking of Flip Wilson, who used to say, 'The Devil made me do it.' That's what I thought. The Devil made me do it."

Ms. Oliver's eyes began tearing. Elvis gave her a tissue.

"I've got a joke," Elvis said.

"Okay, I could use a joke," she said.

"The blonde told the mechanic, 'Oh, my car is dead. Can you fix it?' So he spends ten minutes or so fixing it, and the blonde says, 'What was it?' He says, 'Crap in the carburetor.' And she says, 'Well, how many times a day do I have to do that?'"

Ms. Oliver found that a good one.

The home was pensive and transitive, between the afternoon event in the auditorium and dinner. She sat forward in her wheelchair, her hands folded on her lap. She moved them now and then, exercising them, fighting the aches that wouldn't leave.

Elvis confided that a secretary had been flirting with him. What to do?

She said, "Ask her if she'd like to see *Chicago*. And you know what she'll say? 'I thought you'd never ask.'"

"Yeah, I guess," Elvis said, still timid with girls.

There was a hint of a nod from her. She had a teacherly investment in his development.

Elvis found himself in an uncomfortable zone when it came to girls. Girls his age he found immature. Girls mature enough for him were too old. So he figured it was best if he got his life on the right track first; then he could worry about girls. They weren't becoming extinct was the way he looked at it.

Ms. Oliver cautioned him about flirtations with the wrong type of girls: "Sometimes they want to get pregnant. But a man has to learn to protect himself."

Elvis knew. There were flocks of them in his neighborhood.

On Thursdays, Elvis always filled out her weekly menu, and they combed through the limited options. He knew her tastes so well, he really didn't need to ask; she always took the hot dog and beans, cranberry juice, ice cream every day. Tea was a must.

"So for Monday you have chicken stew, or you can have the tuna sandwich or the veal."

"Give me the tuna sandwich."

"For dinner you have cheese ravioli, or you can have a roast beef sandwich or breaded fish."

"Give me the fish."

"Boy, you are going for protein." He paused. "You know what I'm looking for—your hot dog."

"They may not have the hot dog this week."

"Doesn't look like it."

They sped through the remaining days, their practiced routine.

"You know, Elvis, I try eating salad for lunch, and it doesn't work for me. I need real food."

"Have you been getting your cranberry juice?"

"Yes, I have."

"Good that we made that note."

They resumed their easy chitchatting, the back-and-forth of their simple declarative sentences. They talked about going to the pizza parlor when the weather improved—a modest excursion that meant anticipation, possibility. Ms. Oliver's face shone, the presence of youth enlivening her, the simple power of fellowship.

Then Elvis turned serious: "A friend of mine recently got shot right in the neck. He's alive, he's okay, but he was on the ground, twitching, and it was hard seeing that, someone you're friends with."

"What was it?" Ms. Oliver asked.

"It was a stray bullet," he said. "We don't know where it came from. That goes on in my neighborhood, stray bullets hitting people. And lots of times bullets that aren't stray hitting people. You always got to watch out. But how do you watch out for a bullet?"

She gave a concerned look. "You have to watch yourself,

Elvis," she said. "Soon, I hope, you'll get out of there. You need to live in a safer area. I worry too much about you."

She asked him about Long Island University, whether he had registered and chosen his courses, and he just groaned. Endless red tape, especially with his tuition-free setup, and so it was this form, that form, the everyday weight of reality; it seemed that you needed to go to college just to learn how to enroll in college. He would get it done, he told her, in a couple more months.

Good. That pleased her.

Elvis said he was thinking that after college he might apply to medical school, push his aspirations that far. "The question is if I get the scholarship," he said.

"You would make a great doctor. You know, Elvis, it's important to lead your life in a meaningful way. So you don't get old and say I should have done this and I should have done that. I don't feel that way."

"I have those same thoughts, Miss Oliver, but you put them into words."

"The thing is, don't beat yourself up."

She then changed the subject, mentioning that a researcher from a hospital had stopped by, wanting her to donate her body for research.

"Yeah, I think they do that in every hospital," Elvis said.

"Really, they have a researcher ask for your body?"

"Well, you can say no."

"I've heard they can use the skin of dead people for

something. It's not just your heart and liver and all that that they want. Even your skin."

"I don't know what they use skin for."

"Neither do I. Well, I'm not interested in science. I think science is destructive. One minute it's progress, and then the next minute it's not progress. Like when they made the atomic bomb."

"Yeah, but look at that light. That came from science."

"I could make do with candlelight."

"Yeah, but it might catch fire or something."

"People made do with it. Anyway, I was thinking, the way the world is going, I don't feel they need to save any more people. I almost think that nature is trying to depopulate the world."

"Boy, you're right about that, Miss Oliver."

"When I see how many people have been killed in wars, I realize that must be nature's way of depopulating the world. If there weren't all these wars, there wouldn't be enough food to feed everyone. So I assume it's nature doing this."

"I think you make a good point there. I think you're onto something."

"Do you believe in fortune-tellers, Elvis?"

"I don't think I do."

"Well, I once went to a fortune teller. I was with a friend, and I told her I didn't believe in this. I waited in the car while she went in, but then the fortune-teller came out to me and said she wanted to say something. She said I was trying to go on a trip over water. She said I was recently married, and it was a second marriage. And it was true. I was a widow, and it was my second marriage. And I did go to Europe with my daughter. So I don't know. That really threw me."

Elvis said, "That's hard to understand. But I don't really believe in them. I'll tell you, my friend, he wanted to find out something in the future, so he called up this Miss Cleo that was a phone fortune-teller. He ended up hearing things that he already knew, and he had to pay, like, a four-hundred-dollar bill. That sort of stuff doesn't make me a believer."

"I hear what you're saying. Miss Cleo was someone trying to make a fortune by telling."

"You got that right."

"You know something, Elvis, I don't feel old."

Elvis said, "You don't seem old to me."

The dayroom began emptying out, the low throb of voices evaporating. They gazed out the windows of this place for the old, afternoon sliding toward twilight. Storm clouds threatened in the packed gray sky. Fall on 106th Street.

Ms. Oliver asked him to drape her blanket over her legs. "My legs get cold," she said. "When I was young, I would see people sitting like this with blankets over their legs, and I didn't know why. It's because your knees get cold."

She told Elvis that she had just had her weighing and had gained two pounds since last month. "It's all that chocolate," she said.

She got weighed once a month on a scale at the end of the

hall. First a couple of aides weighed her empty wheelchair; then they weighed her in the wheelchair and subtracted the weight of the chair, a math problem. Month after month, they did it the same way, even though the weight of the wheelchair never changed. It didn't gain weight. It didn't lose weight.

Elvis said, "You know, once in the volunteer office, they had this bet to see who could lose the most weight on a diet. They found the diet, and some others, on this Internet site. One day have two crackers. Have water with salt the next day. Crazy stuff like that. They followed it to the end. Then they noticed the warning at the bottom of the site: 'Do not follow these diets; they're not for real.' And nobody lost any weight, either, and they were eating this awful stuff."

"Well, I'm determined to lose those pounds."

"You've got to watch your figure, huh, Miss Oliver?"

"After all, Elvis, I have to roll myself around."

He gave her an impish smile. "Want to have a Chunky?" he asked.

Ms. Oliver smiled back. "Why Elvis, I thought you'd never ask."

· 8 ·

It was a powerful wind, beating hard against the panes, and it was Tuesday or Wednesday or Thursday, the days a blur inside the home, unable to separate themselves from each other in endless time. She sat with the radio on softly, her eyes half shut. Lunch was all done, the hot dog today, one of her favorites. A successful meal, not too much miscellaneous moaning from her lunchmates.

Hers was a settled spirit. She had never had more than a touch of self-doubt and self-consciousness in her life, summing it up as "just fine." She was at peace with the past, a past she didn't dwell on much, though her conversations with Elvis led her to comb through her memories and secrets, and her history would piecemeal present itself.

Her family name was Robinson, and she was born in Augusta, Georgia, on November 15, 1909. Her father, Bowdry

Robinson, whom everyone called Patrick, was a blacksmith. He was a light-skinned black man, because he had some Irish blood in him, and on Saturdays it was his custom to stop in at one of the bars and get a little tipsy. She would be outside playing jacks, and when he wobbled home, the other kids would joke, "Here comes your Mick father." She got her father's light skin, and that was good in some respects and bad in others.

Her mother, Sally, was a nurse, but she had too many children—four girls and five boys, with a seventeen-year age gulf between the oldest and youngest—to pursue that career after she got married. Margaret was the second oldest. When she was eight, the family, not yet up to full strength, moved to New York. Her parents felt a better life awaited them in the North, removed from the harsh bigotry of the South. Through connections, her father found a blacksmith job in Cleveland, and the family moved there after a few months. She had pleasant memories of Cleveland, the family expanding, a roughly middle-class lifestyle, the joys of riding the streetcars. She was not overly inclined toward religion, or at least she wasn't inclined toward any one religion. Her mother had an innovative attitude that she appreciated. She told the children that they should go to whichever church their friends happened to want to go to that Sunday, and so one week she would show up at the Catholic church and another at the Methodist and yet another at the Presbyterian. It was all so much more interesting and fun than the same place and the same people week after week. After school, she would have friends over, and they liked to have cocoa and they would make taffy pulls. They went to the movies. In her early teens, for reasons that escaped her, Margaret developed a fondness for opera. Her mother got her several opera records, and since no one else in the family had much interest, Margaret would retreat to her room, instruct the others that she was not to be disturbed, close the door, and listen to her opera. Life seemed easygoing and forever.

When she was sixteen, the worst happened. Her mother, only in her late forties, abruptly took ill and died. The doctor's explanation was "complications." After more than three-quarters of a century, the thought of her mother's death was still numbing. Here she was in her nineties, and yet her mother's life, with all those children dependent on it, ended so quickly.

It was impossible for her father to care for so many children, and so he remained in Cleveland with the oldest brother, who was out of school and working. The other eight children were divvied up between two aunts living in New York. A third aunt also lived in New York, and although she didn't absorb any of the children, she helped out financially. The aunt Margaret moved in with was married and had a daughter a year older than Margaret. They lived in Manhattan and later moved to the Bronx.

Some serious sibling rivalry flared between Margaret and

the cousin, even though Margaret did her best to squelch it. When the two of them returned home together from school, her aunt would inquire of them, "So how did you do on the test?" The cousin, not the most stellar student, would reply, "I got a sixty-five." Margaret, who actually got a ninety, would say, "Oh, I got a seventy." She didn't want to show up her cousin, have her think she was smarter than her. Nonetheless, the rivalry built and intensified. There were times the cousin would stare at her, and it was as if a hole were being bored into her forehead.

Margaret grew tired of the tension. Then a fortuitous thing happened. When she was nineteen, she went to visit some friends who had known her mother. They introduced her to the lady living across the hall, who had a daughter the same age. There was instant chemistry. In passing, Margaret happened to mention that she hoped to find somewhere new to live, and just like that the woman invited her to come live with them.

By this point, she had finished high school and was working. She had a job as a buyer for Cathleen, a dressmaking company. She would buy fabrics and then take samples to customers for their inspection. She had found the job by responding to a classified ad in the newspaper, because she had learned to sew in school and always loved it, and wanted somehow to enter the dressmaking business.

She enjoyed the new living arrangement. She became very friendly with the daughter. But her life was moving swiftly toward its next stage. Two years later, when she was twenty-one, she met a young man named Walter Jones at a cocktail party. They liked each other, had some good laughs and engaging conversation. The next day, the man who threw the party called her up and said, "I see you and Walter get along, but I have to tell you he's married. You're a nice girl, and I don't want you to get into something like that." The news took Margaret by surprise; she would never intentionally assume the role of "other woman." When she confronted Walter Jones with the information, he had to laugh. He explained to her that another young woman had been pursuing him, and his lack of interest didn't seem to discourage her, so he finally told her he was married. The man who gave the party heard that from the woman and assumed it was true. Soon Margaret Robinson and Walter Jones were married. The year was 1932.

He had a solid job at the customs service. He was living in Manhattan, and she moved into his apartment. The first month, she got pregnant with twin daughters. Before the twins were born, her father contracted pneumonia and died in Cleveland. Since moving to New York, she had not seen him, and she wasn't able to attend the funeral. The twins were born prematurely, at seven months. One was three pounds, eleven ounces; the other, four pounds. They were fraternal twins. The doctor told her, "They're just sisters born at the same time."

Margaret thought it was important that she stay home and

raise her daughters, so she relinquished her job. The family lived comfortably enough on Walter's salary. She was glad of his government job, because the country had spiraled into the Depression. Many of her friends' husbands had lost their jobs, and the families were really pinched. She remembered the time her daughters went to a party at a friend's house. An investigator from the Welfare Department was there to interview the parents, because they needed to go on welfare. Her husband had to accept a small salary reduction, but not enough that it impacted their lives in any meaningful way.

They moved into a better neighborhood in the Bronx, into what came to be a famous apartment complex called the Coops at Allerton Avenue and Bronx Park East. Coops stood for Workers Cooperative Colony. It was opened in 1927 by a group of workers who embraced Marxism. Earlier, they had organized a cooperative restaurant, a cooperative summer camp, and a small residential building in Harlem. Their success with those attempts led to the more ambitious Coops. They built apartments with soaring ceilings, splashed with sun, just three or four apartments to a floor, and single rooms for the unmarried. For a while, there was a cooperative butcher shop, laundry, and tailor shop, though they were unable to successfully compete against neighborhood counterparts. But a library, nursery, kindergarten, and social and cultural activities prospered. Income at the Coops declined precipitously during the Depression, and in 1945 the complex was sold to a private owner, ending the socialist experiment.

Some depictions of the Coops suggested they were entirely populated by communists, which was not the case. Though decidedly liberal in their outlook, Margaret and Walter were not communists. After all, he worked for the government. They wanted to move to the Coops because the apartments were nice and the neighborhood was an improvement. Walter had to ask permission of his boss at customs before they made the move, and he told him it was fine, so long as he wasn't planning on joining the Communist Party.

Life went well there. Margaret had good friends, and so did her daughters. A lot of weeks, she accompanied three of her girlfriends to Yankee Stadium, where they would have a ladies day, the women getting in for a quarter. When her daughters were thirteen, tragedy visited her again. Her husband died, that time she had the premonition. He had a heart condition as a result of scarlet fever when he was a child, and his exhausted heart simply gave out. He was thirty-nine. When she thought back to that moment, she would say, "I really learned what the word *courage* meant."

Just like that, her finances fell into tumult. She rented out one of the bedrooms in the apartment to a young woman to bring in some extra income, and she went to work. Her daughters were old enough that she felt that they could come and go without her being there. She got a job as a dressmaker in the garment district, and she would also make clothes at home for customers she found by word of mouth, including neighbors. One customer in particular gave her lots of business. One day Margaret was shopping for herself, trying on some clothes at a department store. She noticed a woman shrugging into a dress next to her, and she mentioned that the dress would fit perfectly if she took it in a little here and a little there. The woman asked her, "Are you a dressmaker?" She said she was, and the woman requested her card. She didn't have a card, but she wrote down her phone number for the woman. The woman never contacted her, but she gave the number to a friend, who called and became a steady and devoted customer. That fortuitous encounter, and taking the chance of speaking up to a stranger, did a lot to feed her children.

Until her children were old enough to be on their own, she decided that her social life was of secondary importance. Not that she had no interest in men. Gradually, she took up with an old boyfriend, someone who had asked her out a few times, to a movie and a tennis match, even before she met her husband. He was a counterman at a drugstore. There were some complications. He had a previous girlfriend whom he had gotten pregnant. He wasn't ready to marry her, but she went ahead and had the baby and wound up marrying another older man. Margaret started dating him, and romance flowered anew. She thought he would want to marry her, because she certainly was interested. Time passed, a year, two years, five years—as she would later put it, "He began to seem like an old shoe"—and so where was the proposal?

Things got sticky. His old girlfriend's husband died, and she now started saying that as the mother of his child, she should rightly become his wife, not Margaret. He became more distant. Margaret got the impression that he was buried in guilt. She figured enough was enough, that he was one of those men who would never be quite ready to get married. The affair petered out. He never did marry.

Not long afterward, she ran into someone at a party at a friend's house. His name was Eugene Oliver, and she had known members of his family, in particular his sister, and so she knew he was of good stock. A couple of years older than she was, Eugene worked at the post office in Brooklyn, handling parcel post. They started going out, and she liked him well enough. To tell the truth, there was never deep love there, not like with her first marriage, or even with the man she had been dating. But they got along with some passion and little friction. She didn't want to be alone, and so when he proposed she consented. They were married in 1956. They found a cooperative apartment on Tenth Street and Avenue C in Manhattan, and they bought it. She continued to do some sewing for private customers out of the apartment. It was more of a marriage of convenience. Eugene shared none of Margaret's cultural likes. When she went to the opera or theater or ballet, she did it with other woman friends. That was not for him. He preferred watching sports, which never engaged her. "He liked to hang around the house. He was one of those people." They were quiet years.

She had grandchildren now, and she spent a good deal of time entertaining them, which pleased her immensely. Her apartment building had a swimming pool, and her daughters and their families loved to come over and swim. The marriage lasted for seventeen years, until Eugene Oliver died of a heart attack in 1972. He had the same condition as her first husband, a weak heart brought on by scarlet fever as a child.

Margaret continued to live by herself in the apartment for two more years. She was lonely, tentative about how to fill her days. She developed rhinitis that was awful in the winters. She had to have a vaporizer running all the time. A married couple she was friends with retired to Phoenix. She visited them there and liked it; the climate was good for her rhinitis. She was feeling adventuresome. She decided to sell her apartment and, just like that, move to Phoenix. She would stay there for fourteen years.

When she lived in Phoenix, she had a number of residences. People moved a lot there, contagiously itchy feet, and so did she. At first, she had a furnished studio, but it was too small to suit her. She upgraded to a one-bedroom. Then, through a friend, she agreed to babysit a teenage daughter while the parents went to Europe. They were strict. They had a swimming pool, but the rule was that if boys were over, the girls and boys couldn't be in the pool at the same time. She stayed on when the parents returned, but she felt out of place. She moved in with another woman she knew. The woman died. So she found a studio for herself.

She had never gotten a driver's license but was fortunate to make friends with people who picked her up and took her places. One day a week, she volunteered at the thrift shop of the local animal shelter. She worked the book room. Another younger woman who worked there, named Mary, became a close friend. There was just a natural affinity between them, and they did a lot together. Mary's husband worried about her constantly, and didn't like her being out of his sight, but when he met Margaret he felt Mary was in good hands, and when they were out together it eased his mind. Margaret was friends with three other women, and they would meet once a week to play bridge. They were all good players but not overly competitive. When it came time to have snacks at the end of the evening, it was often unclear who had won.

Men were no longer integral to her life. A woman who lived in the same apartment complex as she did announced to her one day that she was moving to California, and let her know that she had suggested to her boyfriend, who was not accompanying her, that he ask Margaret out. She would speak of him as the boyfriend that she inherited. It was a brief and hardly fruitful inheritance. She had him over to dinner once, and they went out once. She didn't care for his personality, and that was it. "That was all the dating I did," she would say. "I didn't care. I had had enough. Older men are different than younger men. I don't know what it is, but there's something about older men. I guess I always had a young attitude, and these men were more settled. They were sedentary, and I wasn't. But I was just fine on my own."

She realized she was getting older herself. Her children were getting older. Her grandchildren were getting older. She missed them. Her rhinitis was cured. She felt it was time to return to New York, and so she did. As it turned out, the rhinitis began to return bit by bit, never anything like it was, but worse than in Phoenix. Still, she didn't have the cough she used to have, and she didn't need a vaporizer in the winter.

She settled into the Williams, a home for the elderly at Ninety-fifth Street and West End Avenue on Manhattan's Upper West Side. Operated by the Salvation Army, it afforded inexpensive housing for people fifty-five and older who were self-sufficient. At the time she moved in, wheelchairs and walkers were prohibited. She understood that the reason was that they congested the elevators. Margaret had a nice enough room with a bath, maid service, and two meals a day in the dining room.

She lived in the Williams for five years, happy enough with the arrangement. The home boasted a library, a lunchroom, and an auditorium where residents watched movies and performances by schoolchildren. She made some friends there; the place employed a hostess who introduced new residents to the others. She was conveniently located to the heart of Manhattan. She liked to go to the nearby Mannes

College of Music and listen to the concerts. One of her daughters lived on Sixty-sixth Street and visited her frequently.

Arthritis, however, took hold of her. It began in her back, then infiltrated her hands and arms and legs. Suddenly, the simple act of walking became a feat for her. She began to stumble. These weren't outright falls. She thought of them as theatrical falls, because she would find her knees buckling and she would sort of slip to the ground. But she began to fear a serious fall. She knew one bad fall could mean a broken hip or a broken leg, and who knew what sort of convalescence. Getting old sometimes seemed to be entirely about how to stay upright. She began using a stick with prongs jutting from the end to steady her. Still, she would fall. She needed a walker, but the Williams wouldn't allow it. She was reluctant to tell her daughters of her plight; she didn't want to be one of those aged relatives who were a constant burden to their children, one issue after another, woe is me. She began having her meals sent up to her room, and she closeted herself away. She didn't want to fall. It got terribly dispiriting for her. She loved the presence of others, the vibrancy of life on New York's streets, and here she was sitting in her room, day after day. Finally, after a few weeks of this dreary isolation, she couldn't stand it anymore and confided in her daughter Janet, who insisted that she immediately move in with her.

Janet's apartment had three bedrooms, and Margaret was

installed in one of them. She was still fairly mobile, able to get about with a walker and a wheelchair. A home attendant visited and fixed her lunch and took her to the park. Different attendants came during the week, and her experience with them was not favorable. Turned out they stole. Little things, big things. Margaret had a suit bag at the end of her closet, where Janet had stashed her jewelry. One of the attendants swiped the jewelry. Another one took a tape recorder off the piano in the living room. Silverware vanished. The incessant pilferage aggravated her no end, but it seemed impossible to find someone honest.

Increasingly, Margaret's needs intensified, and there was a quickened awareness of her growing dependency. Someone had to dress her and bathe her. The minute Janet entered the apartment, Margaret would be barking her accumulated needs from her day ensconced in solitude: do this, do that. Her reliance on others baffled and demoralized her. She resolved that she wasn't going to become a detested chore to her own children. And her life was constricting at her daughter's apartment. It was hard for her to get out, and entertainment within the apartment was limited: a book, music, television. A young woman, a volunteer at one of the social services agencies, came to visit now and then, and so did another young woman, but she yearned for more interaction. She knew it was time. After living with Janet for eight years, she told her that she wanted to move to a nursing home, where there was always someone to care for her and where there were more diverting activities for her to pass the time. Janet was ready, too. She told her mother, "Mom, if that's what you want."

Margaret quickly made peace with her decision. "People complain about being in the home" is how she would explain it. "This man was complaining in the auditorium. He said he was sick of being here. I felt like saying, 'You're also old.' When you reach a certain age, it's time. We have doctors, lawyers, actresses, all sorts of people here. You have to realize, when you're old you're all the same. You're just plain old."

But her yearning for another day was still there. And so she found her way to Room 470, the bed next to the window, bringing with her just the things she absolutely needed, to live until the end came.

· *9* ·

The auditorium had to be gotten ready for the Friday Sabbath service, which always drew a good turnout. This was part of Elvis's job in the religious services department. It went like this: pull out the lectern and audiovisual equipment, set up chairs for the aides and the more mobile residents able to attend without wheelchairs, then get the refreshments ready, a big part of the draw. It was all routine, something he did week after week without thought. The auditorium was on the first floor, down the hallway from the library and the coffee shop, and so the laborious part was rolling the residents down and afterward rolling them back to their rooms, but he did it with a cheerful insouciance. It allowed him to circulate beyond Room 470, to interact with the home's other residents, to poke along the floors and nod hello, to see what the oldsters were up to. A lot of people came to the service, and he had to move with expedition.

"Hi, Millie, you coming?" he asked a woman seated just outside the door to the auditorium.

She was in a wheelchair; she had no legs. A faint whisper came from the woman. "Don't know," she said. "Still thinking about it."

Elvis nodded at her. He knew there was no rushing her, that the decision could be a long time coming, various considerations colliding. "I'll leave you here at the door to decide."

He took the elevator to the top floor. He heard a ragged scream from some distant room. Walking down the corridor, he peeked into rooms trolling for prospects, coming upon slumping people staring at the TV, others with the radio on, a woman chanting, "I want pants. I want pants," until he found a regular, eager to go. "Let's hit the road," he told her, and she replied, "Yes, hit the road, but not too hard."

By now, the rabbi was in position up front, playing a guitar and singing softly, getting the early arrivals in the mood. When Elvis wheeled the woman in, he handed her a book with the lyrics of the songs, so she could follow along, though not many seemed to do that. His friend Oliver Lora was also helping to round up the congregation. Oliver gave Elvis a knowing look as he steered an old man into the room.

Elvis spotted someone at the door. "Hi, Flo, I have Julie in here. Let me take you to her."

Flo said, "I don't even know who that is."

"Sure, you know who that is."

"Julie? I've never met anyone named Julie. No idea who you're talking about."

"You see her every day."

"Not me, Joe. Certainly not me."

The woman called Elvis "Joe." He didn't know why. She used to call him Elvis, but for some time now she had been calling him Joe.

He got a chair for a woman in a walker. He put her behind a man with an oxygen tank attached to his wheelchair. The woman brought her own cushion with her. Elvis placed it on the chair, fluffed it up a bit for her.

He went up in the elevator to round up some more residents. He got off on three, where a woman was sitting by the elevator with a bag of clothing heaped on her lap.

"Hey, Pearlie," Elvis said. "You doing your laundry?"

In the dining room he found a woman named Edith sitting before the television, a movie playing, the volume cranked up, some old western, the outlaws temporarily having the upper hand. "Hey, Edith, how are you? Tired?"

"Yeah," Edith said. "I'm exhausted."

"Too much partying, huh? You want to go down to the service? Why not? You're not doing anything. I'll make sure I bring you back. That's a good movie, but you're not watching it."

He maneuvered her out to the elevator. Pearl still sat there with the bag of clothes.

Elvis said, "Pearlie, wurlie, you're my girlie."

An aide showed up, and Elvis asked her, "What's with Pearl?"

The aide said, "She's going down south."

"Oh, you're out?" Elvis said to Pearl. "You're bouncing on us."

Pearl said, "Yes."

Elvis said, "I don't blame you. I wouldn't want to be around me either."

Taking Edith down, Elvis was kind of quiet. He mentioned that he hadn't slept well last night. In fact, he never slept well. No matter when he went to bed, he always woke up at three in the morning. There was a reason.

It happened when he was twelve, a week before Christmas. The schools were out for a couple of weeks because of a big blizzard. He was at home, in bed, around three in the morning. He slept in the living room, on a salvaged rollaway, and his parents were still up and his mom turned the radio down so it wouldn't bother him. His stepfather had been drinking, didn't like his music being interfered with, so he kicked her. Elvis had never seen anything like that—his mother hit. It scared him, made his lungs tight. It happened other times, other disorienting moments. From then on, if he heard a noise, he'd wake up with tears in his eyes, and he'd go stand by the bedroom door and try to listen to see if his mom was okay. Now, on his own, he would come home from work bone weary and it might be midnight and he'd fall right asleep, but he'd wake up at three because that was when it happened. Night after night, the same fitful sleep.

He frowned. "I'm a bad-tempered person away from here," he said, after bringing Edith to the auditorium. "When I'm walking down the street, I have to put on a mean, tough, angry look. You have to look like that in the hood, because anyone who lives in the hood has bad memories that don't get erased. When I go to the store to get some food, I remember the time I got jumped four years ago. I got hit in the ribs with a golf club. Four Honda Civics full of guys jumped me. I had got in this beef on the street with this girl. She bumped my friend. They had an argument. I told her to shut up and go home. She told her friends. I was told they were looking for Elvis. They found me. Another memory I have is on 180th Street, where I saw my friend get shot. When I go to the park, I remember I had a fight there. These things add up, and they make you into something you're not. I look friendly when I'm at the home, but you wouldn't recognize me in the hood with my mean face."

He stumbled on another prospect for the services, a redhead he called Gorgeous. "I call her Gorgeous because she must have been gorgeous in her youth. And she's still gorgeous to me." Gorgeous, other plans in mind, passed on the service.

Elvis entered another room. "Hi, Mary. My name is Elvis. I'd like to take you to the Jewish service if you'd like to come."

"I don't think I'd like to come."

"Okay, you look good. Do you feel as good as you look?"

She shook her head. "Not so good. I haven't been well at all. I had heart surgery, you know?"

"I heard that. Well, you look good. You should feel as good as you look."

"Well, I turned on the narcissism."

"I see. That makes sense."

The world outside was going dark. He passed Ms. Oliver's room. She was sitting by the window, listening to opera on her tape player. He waved. She waved.

A woman spotted him and flagged him down. She needed a push to the auditorium.

"Sure, no problem. You can get some cookies. You can eat them or sell them, make some money."

She chuckled. "That's a good idea, sell them."

Elvis paused for a moment and yanked on his pants. "Wait a minute; my pants are falling down. They're always falling down."

"I can't see. You're behind me. I want to see."

"Yeah, I know, everyone wants to see my butt."

He got on the elevator. He said to the woman he was bringing to the service, enunciating clearly: "Gigi, I need you to put your arm inside. Okay, honey, bunny?"

Gigi was noncommittal. The arm hung stubbornly beyond the armrest. Elvis lightly tapped her arm. She recoiled, tucked it in. "Okay, buster, done," she growled.

Gigi was not her name, but his nickname for her. She was one of the first residents he knew at the home, when he first came here at fifteen. He would take her out to Central Park and buy her chocolate, for she had a fierce sweet tooth, and they read the paper together, discussed current events. She was lucid then. Now her mind was gone. She didn't know who Elvis was. She called him "Sidney." Somewhere in her life there must have been a Sidney, but who knew?

"Sidney, what's going on here? It's not right; it's just not right."

"It's okay, Gigi," he said briskly. "We're fine."

"But it's not right, Sidney. You can see that."

Elvis left Gigi to her imaginings and sat down in a chair along the wall to fill out his transport sheets. He relied on code letters to explain whether a resident came or not. $V =$ present. $B =$ bed. $R =$ refusal. $S =$ sick. $A =$ unknown reason. $H =$ hospital. $DC =$ discharged. $Q =$ quarantine restriction. $D =$ deceased.

Finished with the transport sheets, Elvis sat down next to Gigi. Sometimes she got excited, began shouting meaningless phrases. Elvis would try to mollify her, and if that didn't work he would pick up her cookies and take her back to her room, her religious attendance cut short. She came for the cookies, nothing more. He held her hand. She began talking: "When are the cookies being served?" She got louder, wanted to know about the arrival time of the cookies.

"You have to be quiet," Elvis shushed her. "You're in a service."

She calmed down for a moment, then resumed: "You want to go get it, Sidney? You want to?"

Elvis sighed and told her, "We're going to have to go."

He picked up a cup of grape juice, asked her, "How about one for the road?"

"Where's the road?" she said.

He put back the juice, scooped up her cookies, encased them in a napkin, and wheeled her out.

"So, Gigi, you have a couple of cookies there. Rainbow and chocolate. You like chocolate, so here."

"I hate them."

"You don't hate them. You love them."

"I'll hit you."

"You won't hit me. I'd like to see you hit me. How's the cookie? Hard?"

"Yes."

"You've got teeth."

He showed her how his undershirt was longer than his shirt. "See that, Gigi? That's how we dress in the hood."

"Where's the hood?"

"Someplace you'll never have to go. I can assure you of that. Someplace you'll never have to go."

· *10* ·

"Afternoon, Ms. Oliver. I got some new ones. Copies right here for you. Let me know what you think. Read them when you can. They're new." This was what the Poetry Man said to her, speaking in a puffing way, pauses between the words. He had bad emphysema. A portable respirator was mounted on his wheelchair, the answer to forty years of smoking, and he couldn't talk long before hesitating to ingest some oxygen. But he was lucid, not one of those at the point of detachment from this world.

This encounter happened when he wheeled past, a blissed-out look on his face, finishing a long slow morning. His name was Sid Silver. He lived a couple of doors down the hall, rolled back and forth in front of her room all day, going and coming from meals. He wrote poems, making his statements about life, and his daughter photocopied them. He kept batches of his work in a loose-leaf notebook affixed to his wheelchair and handed them out to residents and staff people, tacked them to bulletin boards. He was prolific, having amassed an inventory of something like 350 poems, and he had future ideas scribbled on napkins and scraps of paper.

She accepted the latest productions with a gracious smile and assured him she would give them a look. Truth was, some she liked, others not so much.

She glanced at the top one, titled "Outlook on Life," and scanned the beginning.

To brighten up the world,
a bit,
All working together,
We can make it.

With a little effort,
it can be done.
Just some help,
From someone.

Another one was called "Va-Va-Voom," and began,

So gracious, I am, to see this day,
Yesterday, gone so far away.
Each and every one so new.
Never by itself, it's for every person, too.

Since there weren't many people on her floor she could talk to and who bothered to visit during her selfsame days, she enjoyed the presence of the Poetry Man. Why not? He used to be a cabdriver, was now in his late eighties. Just don't ask him how long he had lived at the home; that wasn't something he wanted to think about. But, no mistaking, it was a good stretch. He wanted to see his poems published, so that they would produce some money for his devoted daughter, generate a monetary legacy he had not yet achieved.

He wrote on a great many subjects, including Father's Day and pregnancy and the beauty of a woman and the power of a smile. He had been writing poems for years. Some of them had dates on the bottom. He was not the kind of person you forgot.

Elvis could hear the Poetry Man before he entered her room. He took some poems from him and asked Ms. Oliver, "You want to go to the garden?" He approached her with a humorous sparkle in his eyes.

"Yes, that would be nice. The sun is out today. Finally, it's not raining."

He was wearing jeans seven times too large, a T-shirt that could comfortably hold four.

The phone chirped, and she swiveled around to reach it. She scooped it up with both hands, clutching it more in her palms than her clumsy fingers, and it was one of her daughters. Right. Right. Yes. Thank you, dear.

Some aides outside the door were chatting loudly; Elvis gave them a censorious look, and they scuttled down the hall. There was always an abundance of noise in the home, booming voices, messages erupting over the public address system, the clatter of wheelchairs and cleaning equipment, and just footsteps, back and forth, back and forth. It was one of the complaints regularly brought to the attention of administrators. It struck Ms. Oliver that the people working in the home spoke louder here than they otherwise would, possibly because so many of the residents were hard of hearing and they just got accustomed to elevating the volume of their voices. Whatever the cause, Ms. Oliver was sensitive to noise. It somehow bothered her nervous stomach. She really had to work hard to try to acclimate herself to it and not get riled.

It was a delicate balance, the relationship with the aides. They dressed and undressed Ms. Oliver, who couldn't put on her socks or all of her clothing. Some items she could get on, but, as she would say, "It would take a year and a day." She got a shower twice a week, her designated shower days being Tuesday and Friday. She could transfer from her wheelchair to the bed, but only if the wheelchair was close enough that she could prop her feet against the cushion before swinging them into bed. Otherwise, an aide needed to lift her legs into the bed. The home employed "floaters," who filled in for sick or overburdened workers. One night, a floater came in as Ms. Oliver was trying to get into bed. She managed to sit on the bed, and the floater moved the chair away, so she couldn't balance her feet against it to swing her legs in. She told the floater, "You'll have to lift my legs up." The floater scowled and said, "I don't have to lift up anything." So Ms. Oliver said, "Well, I'll have to call the nurse and have them find someone else to do it." The floater lifted her legs.

It was true that status was hard to find in the home. The fact that you had money got you little in the way of preferential treatment. Ms. Oliver saw how that rankled some of her neighbors, who had money and were indignant that it meant nothing in the home. A demanding nature tended to work against you. Ms. Oliver had picked that up quickly. She refrained from losing her temper with aides. She was polite, though firm, when she needed something, and that worked ever so much better than the approach of residents who denigrated the aides and were bossy.

Ms. Oliver belonged to the Resident Council, a formal body made up of residents that met every other week and whose primary function was to offer information to the residents and to entertain complaints and suggestions, mull them over, and pass on to administrators the ones they deemed justifiable. They were more often small matters rather than large, pertaining to issues like the persistent noise and the quality of the food. Someone didn't like the meat pie. The bread wasn't fresh enough. Once Ms. Oliver brought up the matter of creamed spinach. She didn't much care for it prepared that way, and wondered why it couldn't simply be served raw. It was tasty and healthy that way. Not much came of that one.

"Elvis, before we go, something I've been wanting you to do. In my drawer I have some opera arias. I'd like you to get some out and put them in the player."

Elvis fished out three opera tapes, different editions of *50 Great Moments in Opera*, and left them out for her. He inserted one of them in the player, so it was all ready to go.

Ms. Oliver seemed unaccountably quiet. He was going to say something about it, but then he decided not to. When they were going down in the elevator, she said her eyes were bothering her, her vision cloudier than it had been. She flexed her fingers, trying to shoo away the arthritis.

They got outside, the sky interrupted by some small cottony clouds, and found a quiet spot. "You know, Elvis, I have no regrets about my life, none at all," she said.

"Really. Well, that's good."

"And I think that's important, to live your life so when you get old you can say that. Because if I did have any regrets, there's not a lot I can do about it at ninety-three."

"No, I can't see where you could."

She asked him how things were going with getting registered for school. Lots of red tape, he told her, getting forms filled out, still straightening out the scholarship he was promised, still making phone calls on top of phone calls.

Espi from the volunteer office, he said, was doing a lot to help him sort it out. College was going to happen; he knew that. Ms. Oliver badly wanted him to do well there.

"Remember, the world won't just offer you things," she said. "You have to go after them. You have to make the first move."

Elvis said, "I hear you. I didn't hear that before. I've been thinking, me and my mom, it's like she knows me but she doesn't know me. I ask her a question, and she doesn't know me that way. My family, I ask a question, I know what they're going to say."

"Well, you didn't have a constant relationship with your mother."

"Now I understand the job was too difficult. It would be ninety-five degrees out, and she would be in her truck. All metal, two stoves and a grill, everything on. It was like two hundred degrees in there. I was there flipping my burgers, and it messed up my eyes. They got all red. People thought I smoked pot. I was flipping burgers."

"You know, a lot of people, they weren't ready to have kids, and they just bought them all sorts of material things. But they didn't raise them."

"Well, I didn't even have the material things."

"It's like I say, champagne dreams and beer pockets."

"Yeah, right. Speaking of champagne dreams, I brought a Chunky for us."

"Well, aren't you sweet? Remember, Elvis, self-preservation is the first law of nature. You have to take care of yourself first."

Ms. Oliver talked about the time she gave one of her grandchildren a card with ten dollars for his birthday. He opened it and sullenly said that another relative had given him twenty-five dollars. Ms. Oliver told him, "Well, I also gave you a million dollars' worth of love, and I don't know how much love there was with that twenty-five dollars." He went to his room and got a stuffed horse and gave it to Ms. Oliver to thank her.

Elvis said, "I wasn't spoiled. My parents couldn't spoil me. But I understand the meaning of things."

She took a piece of Chunky. Elvis put it in her left hand. "That's my bad hand," she said. "I hope it makes it to my mouth."

It did. She laughed.

"See, you laugh. So many people here complain about things and feel depressed. How do you do it?"

"You accept it. I must say, some days when a lot of things go wrong, you end up saying, 'How did I get here?'"

"Yeah, I know."

"Life is not how you make it. It's how you take it."

She said something funny had come to her today. Years ago, in preparation for a trip to France, she was trying to teach herself some French, as was her daughter Janet. While shopping in Macy's one day, they were practicing the rudiments of what they had acquired, having a conversation. Suddenly, in response to something Janet said, Ms. Oliver uttered, "Geronimo." Janet stared at her and said, "That's not French." Ms. Oliver replied, "I know, but I used up all the French I know."

Elvis gave a hearty laugh.

She inquired about a resident down the hall with whom Elvis was friendly. Was he still getting his meals in his room? He hadn't wanted to eat with the others; they were aggravating him too much.

Elvis said, "He has this little theory. He says people are constantly talking to you here, telling you to do this and do that, with their index finger pointing at you. So he says you have to respond by pointing your middle finger at them. He calls this the two-finger conversation. He's always afraid of not getting his way. But he likes his two-finger theory."

She said, "Well, I guess that's an interesting theory. I'm not sure it's going to get published anywhere, but it is interesting."

Thirsty, she asked Elvis for some ginger ale. He poured her a cup and carefully positioned it in her hands. She took a sip, spilled some drops on her blouse, and he attentively mopped them up with a tissue.

She looked around the garden. Then she said, "You know, when the doctor here sees me he says, 'I can tell you have all your marbles.' I guess he sees a lot of people who don't have too many of their marbles. Sometimes I wonder if I would be better off without all of them. You know how Shakespeare said, 'Once a man and twice a child'? Well, there's something to that. You know how you tell a child to do something and they don't do it? I find I'm like that. There are things I know I should do, and I don't do them. There's a basket on the back of this wheelchair, and I've been saying, 'I'm going to take that basket and turn it over on the bed and see what's in it.' Well, I've been saying that for days and days, and I haven't done it. There are a couple of fountain pens I'm missing, and maybe they're in there. It's like children—they procrastinate. There's no sense of urgency. So I feel my thinking is becoming like a child's, where you don't force yourself to do something. You say you'll do it tomorrow. Then tomorrow becomes the next day and the next day and the next day."

"Yeah," Elvis said, "before you know it, you've got stuff in there for months, maybe years, and you don't even know you have it. You might have food growing mold in there; who knows? You want to turn the basket over now?"

"I think I'll procrastinate a little more."

The clock moved interminably toward evening. They did her menu, made sure she ate.

Ms. Oliver said, "When I was raising my daughters, I told them they had to eat some of everything on the plate. They could have more of some things, but they had to eat some of everything. I told them if they didn't, when they grew up boys wouldn't like them. They'd be too skinny, and they wouldn't look healthy."

Elvis asked, "Did that work?"

"Up to a certain age."

She smoothed her skirt. You could hear a quiz show from one of the rooms, someone whimpering with delight, victorious, the celebratory music coming on, true-life bounty to be paid. They had had a blessed, uncomplicated hour, and it was good. They could see dusk approaching through the trees, another afternoon gone, and the clack of the wheelchairs as the others began to funnel inside, following their prescribed routines.

· *11* ·

Sun flooded the room. A freshly scrubbed Ms. Oliver took her usual spot toward the back of the auditorium, on the left side, directly on the aisle. The position suited her just fine, since it was ideal for an early exit, giving her a reasonable head start on the wheelchair rush hour that overwhelmed the stubbornly sluggish elevators and too often got disputatious: "What are you doing? I was here first; get your wagon to the back of the line." "Move that chair out of my way. Move it." "Hey, since when were you appointed president!"

Even in this soporific stage of life, she was sufficiently sensitive to waiting in line, not to mention listening to boorish behavior, that she carefully plotted exits and entrances, not wanting her time wasted. The speaker or singer would be barely into his wrap-up, and she would be surreptitiously rolling backward, on her way.

Today's event was birthdays. Birthday Day happened every month. The home would gather everyone who wanted to come, and whoever was born that month would have their names announced, and the audience would sing songs and earn a cup of ice cream as a tasty finale. One month three of the celebrants exceeded 100 years, topping off at 104, people well worth acknowledging. The big draw, though, was the ice cream.

These events were pleasant enough for her, a useful interlude in her day, a different place to be than in her room, but she would hardly regard them as intellectually stimulating, just light entertainment. In these apocalyptic times, who could object to that?

Uh-oh. She hadn't noticed. That dreaded woman was right in front of her, and it was too late to find a new spot. The woman was always turning around, talking and talking in an amplified clang that seemed to have no end, making it impossible to enjoy the show. If you tried to shush her, she would get nasty with you. Here she was already swiveling this way and that way, chattering with people four rows away. You really had to watch who you sat by. She was displeased at what she had bumbled into, and it gave her a palpitant anxiety .

There was a good turnout for Birthday Day, easily a hundred people. At the front, by the stage, were two tables decorated with paper flowers. Seated at them were the birthday celebrators, quiet, expectant.

The performer was introduced, a middle-aged woman in a red-and-white flowered dress. She sat down at the piano and began to belt out old standards: "I Want to Be Happy," "Happy Days Are Here Again," "Blue Skies," "How About You?" "Sunny Side of the Street," "Young at Heart." You wouldn't want to book her into Vegas, but she carried a nice tune.

There was clapping, stomping, some singing along, though, as Ms. Oliver correctly pointed out, "It's the companions who are making most of the noise."

The songs rolled by: "I Don't Know Why," "Bicycle Built for Two."

The singer said, "We have some good singers here. Some very good singers."

Ms. Oliver chose not to sing, perennially displeased with the quality of her voice. She had a ready explanation: "I say I'm a patron of the arts but not a participant."

Now it was "Seeing Life Through Rose-Colored Glasses." The singer said, "That's the way we should always see it."

Then "Yankee Doodle Dandy," "Auld Lang Syne," "God Bless America."

A few people had fallen asleep. The singer was unperturbed: "Fantastic. You're getting better and better."

The big moment came. All the birthday names were read off. It was a busy month, thirty-six birthdays. Big applause for them, and then the crowd broke into "Happy Birthday."

Napkins were passed out, and here came the ice cream in small white cups. One of the men said gruffly, "I still don't understand. How can you have a party without alcohol? Doesn't make sense. You have a party, you have alcohol."

The show was over. As the residents were wheeled out, the performer sang the final song, "He's Got the Whole World in His Hand."

Soon after Ms. Oliver returned to her room, feeling a little dislodged from herself, Elvis showed up. She filled him in on the birthday celebration, what little there was to say about it. His stomach rumbled. Then, ruminating on how she had lived her life, she said, "You know, Elvis, I got married, reared children. One thing I wanted to do was become a writer. I always had good composition in school. But I learned dressmaking in high school, and after school I took some designing courses at night. Had I gone to college, I think I would have become a writer. I couldn't afford to go to college. My mother had died, and I was living with my aunt. I had to work. I did think about going to college at night, but I was always so tired. I took some tennis classes at the Y at night to learn tennis. I decided my career was being a wife and a mother. And I never regretted that because I enjoyed raising the twins. I enjoyed being a mother. I always say that children appreciate you until age eleven or twelve, and then think you are their persecutor. They always think you're picking on them. I always kept the girls busy so they couldn't get in trouble. I was worried because I didn't have a husband with a shotgun. There's an old joke: Stay away from my daughter, or I'll get you with a shotgun. I enrolled the girls in tennis classes, ballet classes, piano lessons, and they taught themselves typing. I bought Joyce a Fannie Farmer child's cookbook and she learned to cook while Janet practiced her music. I kept them busy through these activities so they didn't get into trouble."

He looked right at her, nodded, letting her know he was in agreement. "That was smart thinking on your part," he said. "I didn't have the activities, so I got into a bit too much trouble."

"Well, you're making amends for it now," she said. "You know, I can't help but think the world is getting worse. The country is almost a fascist country. Every time Congress can pass a law that the president can declare war when he wants, how can you feel good about your country? It's so less kind than it used to be. I remember when my mother used to take a bushel of apples and pears and put it out, and you took what you wanted. A friend said, don't tell me anything about the good old days, but they sure seemed better to me. People today are like a herd of sheep. If it's a new computer or car, everyone buys it. We used to be more individual. What else is worse? The sex thing. They say it's more publicized today. But I feel there's been too much exploiting of sex in the movies and on TV. Children know so much more, and they're not mature enough to handle it. Teachers are accused of abuse. They were always so respected. You have to worry about your children more. Shooting up and everything. I feel bad for this generation. When I was raising my children, I didn't have these worries. More guns, more drugs. In the past, kids separated themselves by their dress. The good kids dressed one way, and the tough kids dressed differently. You could tell. As a parent, you could say, don't play with those kids. Now they all dress the same. Now I guess there are some things better. It hasn't been all straight downhill. People are living better; salaries are better. Computers—one way they're good, one way they're bad. What's going on on the Internet is frightening. Children watching things they shouldn't watch, making acquaintances with people they shouldn't meet. You give your child a computer, and you think they're in their room doing something constructive, and they're talking to some stranger up to no good."

"I'm glad I don't have the Internet," Elvis said. "I don't want to meet anybody hiding behind a screen name. You know, I've really been worn out. I go home, and I'm just exhausted. I'm dying, and I lie down, and that's it."

"Elvis, you need some time off. A day off or a half day off. You better be careful. You should have set hours when you're totally free of this place. You see sick people all the time. You need something else."

She wanted him to get it. Her life was repetition, the big events gone now except for the final one—two months, two years from now, he could be visiting her, and it would pretty much be the same drill; but his life was in front of him, and the choices he made now would foretell the future. She wanted him to hear what she was saying.

Her head ticked back and forth. "You know, Elvis, you

remind me of what we used to call 'mother deaf.' A mother talks so much and tries so hard to give advice that the children tune you out and become mother deaf. I learned that as a young mother. The children are probably counting to one hundred while you're telling them not to steal or to eat their peas. So I tried to tell my kids to use more restraint when they became parents. Maybe I need to use a little restraint with you."

He listened to her gently berating comments, and said, "No, I listen to everything you say."

She made no reply. There were days she thought she was telling him the wrong things, that there was more to him than she understood.

· *12* ·

He appeared in his brother's barbershop. He got his hair cut there for free, the brother discount. Elvis liked to "take a haircut" once a week, or week and a half, spending a lot of time contemplating his hair, practically setting his schedule around keeping it properly maintained. Sometimes, if the place was too busy, he would fall back on a shop on 186th Street and get it cut by a friend he referred to as his cousin. He had known him since they were kids in the Dominican Republic and lived near each other.

Elvis said to no one in particular, "Everyone I know from the Dominican Republic either cuts hair or sells drugs."

Ronny rented the first chair in the narrow shop. On the shelf below the wall of mirrors were his hair sprays, his tonics, his gels, his jar of combs. He was the only barber; the others considered themselves hairstylists. Stenciled on the mirror was the name he went by when he stood before a head with his implements: Ronny Stilo. Downstairs they did manicures and pedicures. Ronny used to work at a shop on 181st Street, where people liked his cuts and his felicitous manner; there were days he would have thirty people waiting for him. Then the shop closed down, and he moved here, and many of his clientele followed.

"He's so good that he once gave me a fade with just a blade," Elvis said. "You got to be crazy to trust someone with just a blade. Man who can do that, you got to respect him; he's got a rare talent."

A blowsy woman with tufty hair bustled into the shop, supporting a tray of fresh fruits, mangos and pears and bananas, seeing if anyone wanted to buy a nutritious snack while waiting his or her turn. A guy looked up from the newspaper, took a banana for a quarter, and that was all the takers. Slow fruit day.

Ronny was giving a fade to a young neighborhood kid, who looked to be about ten. The kid didn't say much, just snuck a glance now and then at what was going on with his hair. His subdued expression gave no clue to his level of satisfaction. A nest of fallen hair grew at Ronny's feet. Tacked to the wall next to the chair was a poster titled "The Dimension of the Style," which depicted a dozen headshots of different cuts Ronny had in his repertoire: a fade, a Caesar, a baldie, a blowout, and so forth. Some of the heads had designs cut into them. When Elvis was still in high school,

Ronny once cut a spiderweb and a spider into Elvis's scalp. When Elvis was in junior high school and on the all-star basketball team, Ronny produced a basketball on fire on his head. People, though, weren't indulging in designs much anymore; not as cool as they once were. At any rate, Elvis didn't figure a decoration in his head would go over especially well at the home, unless he put a wheelchair in it or something like that.

Elvis settled into a chair and watched his brother cut. "I never had that much of a relationship with my brother, because we were almost always separated," he said. "I was living with my mom, and he was living with my father. The first real conversation I had with my brother was three months ago. We talked about how we were separated and how we cared for each other and we would kill for each other, but how our relationship is not too personal. I'll go into the barbershop, and he'll come over and hug me and kiss me, and then I'll sit down and wait my turn. There's a bond, but no strong, loving, driving relationship. Though I always get a good cut."

Walking down Saint Nicholas, his countenance calm, his head looking sharp, he paused to greet the parents of one of his friends, giving them his richest smile. They had a T-shirt stand on the street. Banter back and forth, then he moved on. A warm wind scuttled papers along the curb. He exchanged small talk with someone he hadn't seen in a while, a young guy working in his father's business, delivering wholesale meat. He had only one hand, the other having been caught in a meat grinder when he was four. Elvis went by A. J. Fashions, said hello to a couple of rumpled friends outside. Elvis was wearing a T-shirt that could have been his mom's sleeping gown over baggy jeans shorts; a sweatband encased his head. He wore almost nothing but jeans. He had twenty pairs. All baggy, most of them Sean John and Sports Apparel, the hood uniform.

Outside, under a dusk sky, he encountered two guys haranguing a small man with rheumy eyes and meaty hands. The man was tightly clutching a bottle of wine. Ignoring the torrent of words, Elvis ducked into Villalegre, his favorite restaurant in the hood. It was a beat-up, narrow slice of a place, a counter and five booths. It had a scuffed linoleum floor, and the vinyl booths were shoved so close together it was almost impossible to sit across from someone without your feet intersecting. The place was brightly lit. A blackboard with the specials written in longhand hung on the wall. The ceiling was low and worn. Yet there was something about the place that made it comforting. To Elvis, it was more home than his room. The place was packed, a rubble of voices. Everyone there was a regular. He knew all the faces. The cheeseburgers, he felt, were outstanding.

The owner wordlessly slapped down a plastic-coated menu, not that Elvis needed his memory refreshed, and waited. When a regular hadn't been in for a while and then showed up, the owner liked to welcome him by saying, "Hey, where you been? You just get out?" Elvis ordered a ham-and-cheese sandwich.

He sipped a glass of water and looked over the quiet camaraderie of the place. There was fatigue in his face. He stirred the ice in his water with a straw, thought, stirred. The owner set down the plate with the sandwich. Elvis ate it leisurely.

He climbed the stairs to his room. After work, he often sat outside with friends, hanging out, but didn't feel like it tonight. In his room, he glanced over some of his recent hand-scrawled rhymes, seeing where work needed to be done. He had written:

U can't fight me 1D my
Blows is too fast. I'll have
Modafuka feeling like dey
Surrounded his ass
I'm just not satisfy wit
One blunt o du hush so I doono
How long my lungs
gonna last

He had written:

And I ain't tryin to be
negative das jus how nigga
feel

You'd feel da same way you
got two hold days wit one meal
Or you live by a cruel
Rule and das kill or be killed

Getting there, getting there. Putting aside his notebooks, he flicked on the TV, settling on MTV, taking in the rappers who had made it, the gold jangling around their necks, the smug look of success painted on their faces. Looking good, the rappers looking good.

Another thing: he smoked weed now and then, never too seriously, and he didn't try anything more heavy-duty. His back had been bothering him lately; he had done something to it from the lifting of residents at the home and maybe the residue from all that standing in the food truck. He had smoked three days in a row, just to disconnect the pain from his mind. Self-prescribed medicinal marijuana.

He hated to admit it, but he had sold drugs a little, dabbling in it when there seemed no other way to raise quick money he had to have. He would sell a couple of dime bags of weed, get what he needed, then stop for months. He always saw it as a last resort, an act of desperation. Desperation was a common commodity in the hood.

Since his mom left when he was fifteen, he knew everyone who was doing drugs. A dealer would let him have a half ounce of weed on consignment—that's thirty dime bags, that's three hundred dollars. He paid two hundred, made a hundred. He did that on and off until two years ago. But it was not a job. He did it once to come up with the money to go to see his grandmother. He needed the plane fare. He needed to bring her something, a physical manifestation of his love.

Always, he was careful. He never stood on the corner and sold weed. Instead, he would walk down the street, and if he saw someone he knew who smoked, he'd use the code phrase of the street, "I got that." Or he would say, "I've got that for you to chief." *Chief*, from Indian chiefs who smoked pipes, meant "to smoke."

"I'm not going to sit here and say I'm a criminal. I'm not," he said. "When you have no guidance, it's like leaving a baby on the street alone to walk. I knew what I was doing was wrong. But I had to put food in my stomach. I did a rhyme about it."

To society it doesn't make sense to stand on the corner
Smoking and selling trees.
I'm hungry and I'm making money.
It makes sense to me.

He said, "That goes for all the boys standing on the corner who don't have guidance."

He mentioned a friend of his with a pang of disappointment: "Last night he got dressed up and got together a very good résumé. He has job experience. He went to a restaurant, a new one opening up in Times Square. They looked at him and said we need people with job experience. They didn't ask him a question. They saw his race or his tattoo, I don't know. Later on, he'll probably be downstairs selling some weed. I can't blame him. There's him. And there're people like me. I'm willing to swallow a lot of crap just to get to where I want. I have the home as an example. My plan was to stand on the corner until three in the morning and sell weed. That was my plan until the home came along and gave me an example. But am I going to condemn him? How can I, when he gets put through what he gets put through? What else you want him to do?"

Elvis had complicated feelings about the hood, didn't profess to fully understand them himself. "I will never dislike it. I have a lot of roots here. But you got to worry about getting shot here. You don't see opportunities here. You see violence here. You don't see that you're going to amount to anything. I love the hood, but this is not somewhere where I want my kids to live. When I left the Dominican Republic, I thought it would be a lot better here. That's the way people talked about it. I've been close to death here. I was jumped when I was thirteen. I had a fight with some kid at the 189th Street park. We were playing ball, full court. My ball was on the side, under my hat. This kid took my hat off it and snatched my ball. I thought he was just going to shoot around. But he left the park with it. I chased him out of the park. We had a fight. I stayed at the park, shooting around. Some guy drove up, got out of the car, and shot at me. To this day, I don't know who it was. I just ran, ran, ran. I was trying to outrun a bullet, and that time I did. So someday I want to run from the hood, I do. And I don't want my kids here."

He glanced at the time. His clock radio was twenty-five minutes fast. He set it that way on purpose so it seemed later than it was, to make sure he got to work on time, made it to the home when he was supposed to and didn't keep the old people waiting, the old people with nothing but time but who didn't like to wait.

· *13* ·

Lazy days, nothing happening, not a thing. A mortuary calm to the place. Sylvia stopped by, her companion bringing her over in her wheelchair, into Ms. Oliver's little niche in the maze of the home. Sylvia lived down the hall, in the next wing, well-heeled enough that she could afford a private room and could pay a woman to come by five days a week and push her around and run errands for her. Some days, they would hail a cab and go to Macy's to shop. Sylvia loved to shop.

She was known in the home for being demanding, often complaining about some affront. The other night, she called 911, and the police showed up and found nothing going on, no siege by abductors, no grand larceny, nothing. She was not the only resident to call the police over a peculiar noise or some imagined threat. It went that way in homes.

They got to know each other by chance. From inside her

room, Ms. Oliver noticed Sylvia going by one day and beckoned her in. They talked. Sylvia was good at talking. She immediately liked Ms. Oliver. She excused herself for a moment, saying, "I'll be right back." She returned with some candy and gave it to Ms. Oliver, wanting to start things off right. A relationship was cemented.

Getting this latest visit going, Sylvia said in her adenoidal manner, "Unfortunately, I seem to be having sleeping problems. I'm not sleeping."

Ms. Oliver said, "How's your cough?"

"I still have it. I take this with me." She held up a cup of water.

"I sure enjoyed Trivia today."

"Yes, I did too."

Sylvia mentioned that her blouse was an imitation Christian Dior design.

"Really," Ms. Oliver said.

Sylvia was ninety-four, a year older, and had worked in the garment industry as a stylist and administrator for a maternity company. Mostly, she was involved in marketing. She planned shows. She traveled a lot to Europe. Her mother died quite some time ago, and she used to live with her father and sister, first in Brooklyn and then on the Upper West Side of Manhattan, and kept their apartment after they died. She sold it to pay for her private room in the nursing home and to pay for a companion.

Ms. Oliver didn't believe Sylvia had ever been married,

but Sylvia insisted she had been briefly and was divorced. Once she told Ms. Oliver that long ago she had met a count in England, and he wanted to marry her, and she almost agreed but backed out. She had no children. "That's the saddest thing in my life," she said.

"Sylvia, you didn't go to the college course, did you?"

"No, I didn't."

"They're having a party next week."

"Oh, then I'll go."

"No, you can't. You have to go to a certain number of sessions to be able to attend the party."

"Oh, dear, now I wish I had gone. I love the ice cream at those parties." She started coughing. "Oh, Jesus, get me some water," she said to her companion. "I have a dry throat," she said. "It's really not being treated right."

After taking a drink and regaining her composure, Sylvia said, "I love to dress up, to put on a nice dress. I'm thinking of going to the stores tomorrow."

Ms. Oliver, who ordered most of her clothing from a catalog in Arizona, said, "I never used to wear pants. You would never catch me in pants until my daughter brought me a pants suit when I went to Phoenix. So now I wear slacks all the time because of my knees. They get cold."

Ms. Oliver then changed the subject, saying that at breakfast Elvis turned the station in the dining room to WQXR, her favorite, clicking off the rap station that the aides preferred. "That Elvis is a doll, isn't he?"

Sylvia said, "Oh, I love him. He's delicious."

Both of them were opera buffs and would sometimes listen to an opera together on Ms. Oliver's radio. Unlike Ms. Oliver, Sylvia often would sing along. "I can reach the high C's," she pointed out.

"You should have tried to sing if you can reach the high C's."

Sylvia said, "Well, I had an incident. Many years ago I went to the opera; this was when I was thirty. They played the 'Star Spangled Banner' very rapidly. I was the last one to be singing, '. . . of the brave.' It was the funniest thing. And the audience turned around and stared at me and applauded. So I made my debut. During intermission, I went to have a cocktail. During the performance, there were two elderly people in front of me. At intermission, one came up to me and slapped me with her program and said, 'Why didn't you study voice?'"

Ms. Oliver pondered this and said, "That was certainly odd."

Conversation got sparse. Sylvia decided to go. She said, "I'll give you a tinkle tomorrow."

When Elvis came, Ms. Oliver was feeling a little torpid but suggested they go down to the garden. First, the straps on her wheelchair were loose; could Elvis adjust them? He bent down behind it and found he needed to undo some knots on the straps.

"It's like four Boy Scouts knots."

"Were you ever a Boy Scout, Elvis?"

"No, they had the Boy Scouts in the Dominican Republic, but you had to pay to belong and we didn't have the money. But we knew all the stuff they learned before they learned it. The Boy Scouts would come to us and ask us how to tie knots and stuff."

"You know, one thing kids don't do anymore is climb trees."

"I used to do that to get fruit to sell for candy. One time we were knocking down avocados from behind a church. They had these watch guards there. They were allowed to carry guns. We were knocking the avocados onto the steel roof of a nearby house. This dog started barking and the security guard didn't know what he was shooting at, but he started shooting and shooting, and we ran and ran."

"They should let people have the fruit, not go and shoot them. They can't use it all."

The garden was pretty crowded for an overcast day. They passed another resident named Betty, who was sitting with her sister. Betty said, "Oh, Margaret, it's so good to see you." They were in different buildings and hadn't seen each other in a while.

"I was at your 101st birthday," Ms. Oliver said.

"Oh, great, thank you."

"You're looking well, Betty."

"Thank you." And she did. Her sister came to the home about four months earlier. She was furious when she checked in, cursing everyone out. Now she seemed to have settled down. She was only a few years younger, maybe ninety-eight or ninety-nine. She didn't look it either.

Ms. Oliver said to Elvis, "I'll tell you a story about her. She was a smoker, and her husband used to say, every cigarette, that's another nail in your coffin. Well, she has emphysema. But she's 101. He's dead."

They sat by the goldfish pond. The hospital dog wandered past, looking mangy, as always, but with a spirit about him. Ms. Oliver said, "I heard an interesting discussion about Benjamin Franklin on the radio."

"What about him?"

"Well, he was against slavery, but he had slaves."

"I never understood that."

"He was quite a scientist."

"Isn't he the one with the kite and lightning?"

"Yes, he's the one. You know something interesting. I once went to Thomas Edison's museum, and there was the smallest lightbulb and the largest lightbulb. And there was this tree that was so big you could live in it. I forget what country it was from. I never heard anything like that."

"A tree you can live in. It must have a lot of bugs."

She clucked her tongue and said, "Did I ever tell you about meeting Miss Kitty?"

He gave a dull, puzzled look. "No, I don't think so," he said. "Who is Miss Kitty?"

This was when she lived in Phoenix. She volunteered at the Arizona Animal Rescue League, a "no-kill" shelter that got many of its animals off the euthanasia list at other shelters. One of the founders and board members was Amanda Blake, famous to Ms. Oliver and many others as the redheaded

Miss Kitty, the sultry proprietor of Dodge City's Long Branch Saloon on the TV series *Gunsmoke*. To raise money for the shelter, they held bake sales and dog shows, and Miss Kitty was always on hand, friendly and civil as could be. Her real name was Beverly Louise Neill, and she had been a telephone operator before making it in show business. She had a deep affection for animals. At her Phoenix estate, she kept a lion and ten cheetahs.

What happened was she got divorced and married a man much younger and moved to California. One day, just months after she had left, Ms. Oliver read in the paper that she had gotten divorced again because her husband had contracted an incurable illness. The story didn't divulge any further details. It occurred to Ms. Oliver that perhaps the man knew he was going to die, and he wanted his money to go to his family, not to his new wife. But that wasn't it at all. The man had AIDS and had given it to Miss Kitty. She returned to Phoenix to be with her friends, and within a year, in 1989, she was dead. Ms. Oliver thought that that was such a horrid way for her life to end, such a kindhearted person.

"Think about that, Elvis, she was younger than me, famous, had plenty of money, and she had to die like that."

"Yeah, you can't tell how you're going to die. But everyone's going to do it."

She asked Elvis if he had heard of the song "Turn the Beat Around," a big disco hit in the 1970s.

"I think I have."

"Well, that song was sung by Vicki Sue Robinson, and she was my niece. She died of cancer when she was still pretty young."

"All these people dying before they're supposed to," Elvis said.

"Yes, and here I am, going on and on."

"Like the Energizer Bunny. Funny the way things work."

"The brain is so funny. You'll remember something, and then it will go away. Young people today know so much more than when I was young. It's so amazing. I was in church once and listening to the choir. I was sixteen. I was with a friend, and she mentioned something about sex. I said, 'Only certain people do that.' Can you imagine that? I was sixteen and thought only some people did sex and others didn't. Sixteen-year-olds today know everything there is to know about sex. It's all over the TV."

She shook her head. Across the pond, a relative was showing a photo album to an old woman, a shawl around her neck, flipping pages, pointing at particular snapshots, carrying on a one-sided conversation.

The relative halted at a photo of a young man in a military uniform and fished for flashes of memory.

"Who is this?" Nothing.

"Can you see it?"

Nothing.

"Jay. Your son."

"My son?"

"Yes. He's not with us anymore. But your son. He was a very good son. A wonderful, wonderful son."

"My son?"

It had gotten harder for Ms. Oliver to read. The glaucoma in her eyes had become an increasingly prickly discomfort. Bright light was important. It almost always seemed dark to her. Her good friends Paul and Esther Abramson had brought her a high-wattage reading lamp for her night table. But even with the lamp, she was now having trouble with her large-print books. She had given up reading the newspaper. The type was too small.

Apropos of nothing, she said, "You know, I've been thinking about suicidal people. They're the most courageous people of all. See, I was trying to figure out what this world is about in my old age. And I was thinking of these suicide terrorists. I was thinking about this girl blowing herself up. I wasn't considering the act. It's terrible, the cause. I was thinking about the motivation. Is it any different than a soldier who goes and dies in a war? She's doing it because she wants things to be better for others. Then I started thinking about old people. And if someone is unhappy and very sick, why should they prolong their life if they don't want to? They're going to die anyway. They're just dying a little sooner. So I believe in assisted suicide. Why shouldn't there be that option? I told my granddaughter that if my condition worsens so much that I'm just lying here, I'll join the Hemlock Society. She said, 'Why, Grandma, if everyone decides to do that, who would be there at the Hemlock Society to greet you?' I had to laugh at that. Now I know I wouldn't have the nerve to kill myself. Someone else would have to do it. But I haven't had any discussion with anyone."

"Some reason you telling me this?" Elvis said, playing with his lower lip.

"No, no, I'm just telling you how an old woman was thinking."

"Okay, good, because I was getting a little worried listening to this."

Elvis read her the mail. Resident Council minutes. Last week, Ms. Oliver suggested that strips be put on the floor to prevent falling. Another resident wanted bulletin boards in the hall placed at wheelchair height so they could be seen better. Ms. Oliver also requested that volunteers read to the residents.

Elvis said, "You know, feelings, when you say someone hurt your feelings, that's not really true. You're making it that someone else's opinion is more important than your opinion. If you feel your feelings are hurt, you let that happen. I learned from that. It worked for me."

She said, "First, you have to like yourself before you like others."

"Miss Oliver, I gave this homeless guy in the subway ten dollars."

"Elvis, now you know you can't afford to."

"I don't know. He had no fingers. And he had a cast on one leg. I think I did a good thing. He told me he lost his fingers because of frostbite. He was sleeping outside. I don't know. I couldn't pass him without doing something."

"I think we'll have some Chunky."

Elvis broke it into four pieces. He took one and gave the other three to her.

"I've got a problem," he said. "I have a short fuse for annoyance when someone doesn't do something right. It really annoys me. So I admire your attitude. You can laugh at things. I can't. I get annoyed."

"Remember, Elvis, you can't change people. They have to change themselves."

They got around to talking about illegal drugs.

She said, "Years ago, doctors prescribed some of these drugs for you. It was okay. Not now."

"It seems to me more and more drugs come out all the time. They combine drugs."

"You know they say if they take the profit out of drugs, people wouldn't rob and steal."

"I remember talking about that in school, about legalizing drugs."

"What new drugs are there?"

"There's this drug, zip syrup. It originated down south, and it's come up here. I know a lot of people take it. It's cough syrup with drugs in it. They call it zip syrup. There's a rap song about it."

Elvis's eyes skimmed back and forth at the other residents, lost in thought. He didn't say anything about his own occasional involvement in drugs. Instead, he mentioned one of his friends. "I ran into him yesterday. He has cancer and had to have his leg amputated below the knee. He came over to my place, and we rapped for a while. I told him he was very courageous to keep going. He smokes all the time because he can't deal with it. I told him he shouldn't give up like that. He has to get more chemotherapy, or he may lose more of his leg. He's depressed, and so he smokes."

"I guess he has a lot on his mind."

"He's a good rapper. I don't want to see him give up."

"The thing I find, if you're depressed, you should take a long walk, and it clears your head."

"My friend was telling me he saw this guy in the elevator, and his leg would jut out every time he took a step. So he said, 'Do you have a prosthetic leg?' The guy said, 'Yes, I've had it six years, and I still can't walk right. How long have you had yours?' My friend said, 'I just got a year with this one, and I'm walking fine.' The guy said, 'You're the lucky one, got a good fake leg.'"

"How old is he?"

"He's about nineteen or twenty."

"What kind of career is he planning? Is he going to school?"

"I don't think he is. I think he's counting on rapping. I've got to say, he's good. From his situation, the stuff that's happened to him, he has a lot to rhyme about."

"Can he get his songs published?"

"That's the issue. It's very competitive. It's like Biggie

Smalls said. He's a rapper, and he said to get out of the hood you have to rhyme or have a wicked jump shot. It's one or the other—rapping or basketball. But it's hard because it's competitive in both."

"You're getting out with old people."

He nodded. "Yeah, I guess that's right. Leaving the hood with the old people. I don't need the deadly jump shot, just the right moves with the wheelchair."

Elvis got her ginger ale and poured her a glass.

"Did you take some change from the room?" she said.

"No, I had money. It's all right."

"Elvis, I'm going to spank you."

"I'd like to see that. I'd really like to see that."

· *14* ·

Days, then weeks. Same old, same old, until he hit her with
the surprise. Looking at her with soulful eyes, Elvis said he
wanted to talk. He was fidgety. He had something important
to say. It was a secret, and he got right into it; he had gotten a
woman pregnant, and he wanted to see what Ms. Oliver
would say.

He sped through the particulars, a tightness in his throat.
He knew the woman from his neighborhood, someone he
would run into on the street, and she had been flirting with
him for some time, doing what she could to catch his eye.
He didn't really have an interest. She was fetching enough,
all right, personable with an assessing gaze, but she carried
some heavy baggage. She was older, twenty-six, and had
been linked with someone else Elvis knew, a shadowy guy of
suspect fidelity, and had three kids, all apparently by him.

Now she and the kids were living with her mother. She worked down in the financial district, cooking meals in a corporate cafeteria, being good at executing recipes. Sometimes she'd hang out with Elvis and his friends, group stuff, watch the boxing matches together. One night a bunch of them were over at Elvis's sparse room, listening to music, rapping, drinking. When the others left, she stayed. Before long, they found themselves entangled in bed. One of those things.

"Well, she's pregnant," Elvis said.

And so there it was, he unwittingly a prospective father, trying to see for himself what it might mean, looking for her interpretation.

Oh. Her brows knotted in perplexity. He had her interest. An old woman who had heard it all absorbed the information, then said, "That's some news."

"Yeah, I know."

"It's sort of unexpected," she said.

"For me, too."

"Well."

"Yeah."

"Have you talked about abortion?"

He knew that question was coming. Had to.

After a few bloated seconds, he said, "Yes, we did. I brought that up. And she said she would get one. But she went to the doctor and got cold feet and couldn't do it. She's now five months pregnant."

"When did you find out?"

"Not until she was, like, four and a half months."

She nodded. She understood this drill. "You know, Elvis, if a man doesn't want to be a father, he can't depend on the girl. He has to depend on protection."

"Yeah, I see that now."

"I've told you that before. They say, advice is wasted on the youth, and now I can see it is."

His eyes went to the floor with the sting of that. He said, "No, I just made a stupid mistake."

She asked him, "What are your feelings for the girl?"

"I don't have any feelings. I've told her that. She knows I'm not going to marry her or anything. It was just one of those things that happen. Too much to drink, you know."

Ms. Oliver, working this development over in the tumblers of her mind, decided that this was no demonstration of machismo but that the woman had trapped him, sucked him into a marriage trap. He acknowledged that possibility, her wanting to go someplace he wasn't ever willing to go, but he didn't want to dwell on it, be mad and have that warp his feelings toward the baby. He didn't want to resent the child. Someone started playing the upright piano in the corridor, that same song, whatever it was, that she played almost every day.

Quiet for a moment, pitched forward in her wheelchair, Ms. Oliver looked at him. "Well, you have to keep a distance. If you're around someone all the time, that's when you get in trouble. Guilt is a funny thing, especially when there's a baby involved. Let her take care of the baby. What the baby needs is for you to continue your education, and then you can give it something."

"I know that. But I feel excited about the baby. Now I'll have something to love."

"That's good. You haven't had that. But when people create a child, they have to realize they have an obligation to do right by the child."

"I realize that. And I realize I made a stupid mistake, and I won't make it again. I'm not going to become like my brother."

She hoped that was true. They talked some more, Ms. Oliver issuing cautions, putting up the red flags. He had come so far, and she worried that a child might disrupt his progress, send him plummeting back to his former dismal existence.

She said, a softness in her voice, "You know, Elvis, self-preservation is the first law of nature. You have to take care of yourself first."

There was a tappity-tap at the door. One of the evening aides stopped their discussion, coming in to turn down the two beds. Hi to her. Hi to him. All done efficiently, and then it was just them again.

This was a day in her life, and it was on to routines, doing the weekly menu, checking the mail, and then she turned to a new subject.

"Have you read the Bible, Elvis?"

"Not all of it. It's very contradictory."

"Well, who wrote it? People like you and me wrote it. Humans."

"The theory of mankind to me is that men fear what they can't conquer, and whatever they can't understand they're prejudiced against and hate. I've come up with this from my own life. For instance, I've always wanted to be on top, but if I can't conquer something, I take it out on myself and I've gotten scared. I've tried to overcome that, and to some extent I've succeeded."

"You have because you're disciplined. You know, you're supposed to follow the Golden Rule, do unto others what they would do unto you. But a preacher gets up and carries on and tells you what to do. Who empowered him to get more respect than someone else? I think religion is too political."

"Definitely it is."

"Who is anyone to tell anyone else how they should lead their lives?"

"Definitely. Who is anyone to go into someone else's bedroom or anything?"

"What do you believe, Elvis?"

"I grew up with my grandmother going to church and taking us. I used to go because we got ice cream afterward. That was my grandmother's way of getting us to go. But I think I believe in a higher being. There's something else there. I know a lot of people who go to church, and by putting twenty dollars in a collection basket they think they'll go to heaven. I don't believe that, that you buy your way to some sort of ultimate salvation. I don't believe in formal religion. That may be good for kids to show them the way to live, but it does nothing for me."

"But they should relate it to today. Why are they telling us about things that happened fifty thousand years ago? Religion is just not logical. They tell you there's the Devil and the Creator. When you get old enough to figure it out, you think: Well, where's the Devil? Who created the Creator? It just doesn't make sense to me. When I was young, I went to church and Sunday school, and I didn't think much about it. I read parts of the Bible, and the whole thing never made sense to me. I wasn't brainwashed like so many people are today. So when I got older, I never went to church."

He mulled that thought over in his mind. "Yeah, I hear you. You want things to make sense, or you're going to look for some other explanation."

"Exactly. When I was a child, I prayed for things to happen. Never as an adult. My feeling is so strong that no one can convince me otherwise. It's against all I see. Like I see gangsters going into the Catholic church. I raised my daughters with no religion. I think religion has done more harm than good, if you ask me. I wonder, Do people really think they're going to heaven? I guess they must."

"Yeah, I suppose they figure that. Why else are they praying? I believe if you live righteously, you'll be okay."

"Elvis, what do you believe happens after death?"

"I think you just die. God gave us an opportunity to be

part of the world. We're supposed to do something on the earth. Then when it's time to go, we go and someone else replaces us here. I hope there is a heaven, but I don't think it makes too much sense."

"I don't know anyone who has been there."

"Me either."

"You know, there's this story about a man on death row. He's about to be executed, and the priest asks, 'Is there anything you'd like to tell me?' And the man says, 'Yes, I'll soon know what you've been guessing about.'"

Elvis laughed heartily. "That's a good one. Where did you hear that?"

"It was in a movie."

"When it comes to religion or politics, Miss Oliver, I don't discuss that with anyone else but you. People get too emotional about these things."

"Yes, a lot about this world is crazy."

"Except there's us. We're sane."

"Well, let's hope we are, because somebody's got to be sane."

There was coughing down the hall, the addictive drone of TVs. Well, they had settled some things. Elvis was becoming a father, and there was no God.

· *15* ·

She started with countries. There was Canada, England, Switzerland. She recited these names to herself, ticking them off as rapidly as they came to mind.

There was France, Italy, Mexico. Oh, yes, there was, of course, the United States. That was seven. Not that many by some standards, certainly light traveling for modern-day jet-setters, but pretty good, she thought, a healthy number. Yes, she had seen some things, made the world seem less foreign by travel, farness becoming nearness. Margaret Oliver, bon vivant.

She moved on to states. The first ones came quickly: California, Arizona, Florida, New Jersey. She paused a moment, searching hard. Then: Maine, Massachusetts, Vermont, Georgia, New York. That must be it. Not a bad collection.

Nine in all.

She tried to place some memories along with the destinations, things she saw, people she was with, a snippet of conversation, flesh the scene out, make it more real. It was hard, her brain getting a solid workout.

This was her morning. Lying abed, in limbo. She had awoken at 7:00 or 6:30 or whatever—she couldn't quite make out the clock on the wall—shaken out of sleep by the familiar ramblings of her roommate: "Where are they? Are they coming? Where is everybody? Do you see them?" And then a stream of inaudible murmuring. The unimpeachable signs that a new day had begun.

Then came the wait in the penumbral dawn until the aide assigned to her wing stopped by. You never knew; it could be soon, or it could be a wait. Up and at 'em didn't work in this place. She could swing out of bed unassisted, but that was about it. She needed extra hands to get dressed and make her way into breakfast, get the day going. Where was she, where was she? Usually there was at least a slight wait, lots of people to get started. Not much she could do but lie there, cross her fingers, and think. Easy, of course, to drift into nostalgia, into woe is me narratives, but she resisted those temptations, not wanting to be led into sadness. She invented memory games, working to keep her intellectual firmament sharp. The other day she named the operas she had seen, and threw in the arias. Today she went with how many countries and states she had visited in her travels.

Through the flashing recollections of her trips, she found solace. The time passed. A mellowness came over her.

Not every day started like this, but enough did.

She had had a good dream going last night. She had been invited to somebody's house for a dinner party, and all these people were sitting around, and there was a wonderful assortment of food cooking in the kitchen. Someone announced it was time for dinner. Then an aide came in to give her eyedrops and woke her up. Some timing! That made her so mad. She never got to taste the food. She wished that she could sneak back into the dream, but it was of course gone.

Boy, she wouldn't mind a candy now, but her stockpile was out of reach, over on the window ledge in the wicker basket with the top in the shape of a cat's head.

She glanced out the window, getting bright, dawn leaking in, some wind coming on hard. Outside seemed far away, where people were starting their jobs, making and selling things, where news was occurring.

The aide finally came—"sorry to keep you waiting"—and Ms. Oliver was up and into her circlings, breakfast, a shower, some TV, lunch, down to the auditorium for sing-along, and back to her room.

Elvis came. She was feeling loquacious. She told him about her early morning geography count.

"Boy, that's a lot of places," he said. "I can't imagine going to that many places." He had been to New York and the Dominican Republic; that was it.

"The other day I was counting how many operas I heard. I counted ten, and then I tried to remember the arias. Verdi was my favorite opera composer."

"Verdi, huh?"

"And I love Tchaikovsky."

"What's his name—Tchaikovsky?"

"Yes, he's Russian."

"Sounds very Russian."

"They say you should keep using your brain. So I try to remember things. If there's something particularly interesting I see on TV about a country, I act like I'm a student. I try to remember it by saying it to myself. I say I must remember this fact. I can't read the paper, and I certainly don't have any discussions here with anyone about current events. So I have to get my news from C-Span and other TV shows. I've been trying to remember the different countries on the news—Afghanistan, Iraq, and Pakistan. I also try to remember some things in the past. Like when I was in Europe. I try to remember some of the things I saw and the places I went. I tried to do some crossword puzzles when I got here, but my handwriting is so bad and I couldn't tell what I was putting in where."

"Yeah, I guess that would make it tough, not knowing what was where."

"I got such a fright today. The sun was very strong, and I was looking at the TV, and I couldn't see any figures. I thought I had gone blind. Then I looked to the side, and I could see the numbers on the clock, and I knew it was the sun. When it got weaker, I could see the TV again."

"That must have been scary."

He had noticed she hadn't been reading much, not asking him to help her get large-print books from the home's library, all of this starting to worry him, and she admitted that her eyes were betraying her, worse than they had ever been. She was taking new drops for glaucoma. She had numerous blind spots in her vision.

She looked at the calendar and spoke in a small voice: "I can see that twenty-five as plain as anything. I can see the clock. I can see that building out the window where the light is shining on it. But I can't see dark spaces in the room. If it's all white or all dark, everything blends together."

In lieu of reading, she had been getting books on tape and listening to them: Hillary Clinton's book, Queen Noor's, *Seabiscuit, A Beautiful Mind, The Da Vinci Code,* quite a selection. He hoped she wasn't going to get any worse, tried not to dwell too much on that subject.

Sid Silver, the Poetry Man, dropped in with his daughter and left some new poems. One was "This Summer Is a Bummer," and the other was "July 4th."

Ms. Oliver was wearing a bright spring dress today, looking vibrant, younger than her years, maybe seventy-six, seventy-eight tops. Elvis liked the dress, telling her she looked really pretty and cheery.

"Oh, stop flattering me," she said.

"I'm just stating facts."

"People are always telling me how good I look for my age. I was thinking, When I die, they'll say, 'What a nice corpse.'"

"That's not happening for a good long time."

"I had this red blouse that I wore for two days, and I wanted to wear it again. The aide said, 'No, you can't do that; people will see you and think I'm not taking good care of you.' So she put this dress on me. And you know, I don't recognize it."

"It's yours. I've seen it before on you."

Elvis looked at the hand and arm exercises on her wall, and said, "You know in all the times I've visited you, I've never seen you do any of those exercises. I don't think you do them."

"I do, too," she said. "I do them every day."

"Yeah, right, how do I know that?"

"I'll do them right now."

That said, she swiftly undertook her regimen, lifting her arms with gusto, stabbing the air with them, chortling as she went through her drills.

Elvis slouched on the window ledge, leaning back on his elbows, and watched, amazed, a grin on his face. He howled triumphantly and slapped his hands together. Ms. Oliver laughed at his delight.

"Man, you're good!"

"That's right, I am."

"Go, girl."

"I'm going."

The day being an acceptable one, they headed down to the garden. Next to the entrance was a big glass cage with branches occupied by zebra finches and cockatiels, birds to relax the residents. Most of the birds were content on their branches, sitting idly through another afternoon, though a couple were flitting about, and there were a few residents gathered there studying their movements. Elvis and Ms. Oliver sat near the babbling brook, with the goldfish. They watched the fish.

Ms. Oliver said, "I have a funny story to tell you, Elvis. You know when you have a lot of leisure time you think of things? I was going to a dentist years ago in Manhattan. I was young, about nineteen years old. He made me the last appointment on a Saturday afternoon. There was nobody there. I paid my bill and all, and I went to the ladies' room and got ready to go. And he attacked me. He started kissing me and all. I said, 'Oh, I'm feeling dizzy,' and he hesitated, and then I said, 'You know, doctor, you didn't have to do that. All you had to do was ask. I've always admired you. Could you get me a glass of water?' When he went to get it, I collected my coat and started to run. He got back in time to grab my jacket. Then a man was coming out of the elevator, and I said, 'I'm ashamed of your behavior.' And he let me go. Years later, maybe eight years, I was visiting a friend in New Jersey. It was time for me to go back to the city. My friend said, 'Oh, Doctor So-and-So is taking his little boy to the train; he'll give you a ride.' When I saw him, I said, 'Oh, we've met before, many years ago.' He didn't say anything. Then we came across some boys who were playing in the street. And the boy said, 'Daddy, run them over.' And I said, 'Like father, like son.' He didn't say a thing, not one thing."

Elvis said, "That's something. So you took a long trip down memory lane."

"Yes, during all that waiting in the morning for someone to come along, I think, and stories come back to me. Some of them surprise me."

A number of the patio tables had green-and-white striped umbrellas unfolded over them. Flowers and trees and some benches around the perimeter. A lovely setting, pleasant at any age.

She asked him for an update on college. He gave her a capsule rundown, that he had finally penetrated the bureaucracy thicket, that everything was in order except money for books and some sort of computer to do his papers. The home promised to help on that score. Anyway, he was ready to start the following month. She said that was fine, just fine.

She said to him, "It must have been very tough in your country."

"Oh, you bet it was. Did I tell you the story about the coconut man?"

"I don't think so."

"We were having this funeral for a very well-liked lady in the neighborhood. A lot of people would go to funerals because they gave out cookies and coffee. So they had this funeral, and we were on the way to it. I was eight. In front of the cemetery, there's this guy with coconuts that he's cutting up and selling along with sugarcane. He was always at this same spot for years. Then this other guy comes with an ice cart, and he's going to sell flavored ices. The coconut guy was mad that the other guy was messing up his business. These guys were very poor and very stressed. You take someone's business, and you're taking food from his children. So this fight broke out. The guy with the coconut knocked the ice guy down. He humiliated him. He taunted him. The ice guy knocked down the coconut guy. He went to the coconut guy's cart and got his machete and sliced the coconut guy's head off. I couldn't stop looking at it. Can you imagine that?"

"Oh my goodness."

"There was always a lot of jacking and holding up people there because people are hungry. If someone sees you 'rocking your chain,' meaning wearing it outside your shirt, they rip it off. Two guys will drive by on a moped, and the guy in the back will pull it off. Once I was playing dodgeball here outside the junior high school, and a guy ripped my chain off. Pulled a knife on me."

"It sounds like your neighborhood here, too, doesn't it?"

"Yeah, in fact there are guys in my hood that are known as the Player Haters. If you have some nice gear on, they want to jump you. See, if you have nice gear, you're a player. The Player Haters don't like that. They jump you. I deal with that all the time. A lot of the trouble that starts in neighborhoods like mine starts for the dumbest thing—jealousy."

"Do you go to parties up there, Elvis?"

"Nah, I don't have the time or the interest. You see the same kids you see all the time in the neighborhood in one place. I don't want to see a lot of them. I avoid some streets because I don't want to see some people. So why would I go to a party? And there's always going to be a Player Hater, and I don't need the trouble. I don't want to go to a party and risk being shot. I'm also a lonesome guy. I don't like being with a crowd."

He showed her his right wrist. There was a small tattoo of a Chinese symbol that meant unity. It looked roughly like a square inscribed inside a C. He and four of his close friends got them together, as a bond, soon after he had his little episode in the psychiatric ward. They had all gone through hardships, and they supported each other, a magical geometry among them, and the tattoo was tangible evidence of their intent to always be there for each other and to try to live a proper life. They wanted something else, and to avoid the danger of going nowhere; they hadn't been perfect about that, but they tried. He said, "At first there were three of us, me, John, and Delto; then we invited two others, Gary and Shamir. All of us had to be responsible and doing the right thing. We were all determined to do the right thing and not sell drugs and get off the street. Delto was our example. He always had the best sneakers, the best jewelry, and he never did anything bad. He always worked. He spoke to us about working and not doing drugs. He got a job at the Fairway supermarket, and he worked hard at Fairway, and they gave him a supervisor's job. He's been at Fairway for eleven years, and that's a long time at one place for a guy from the hood, so he must be doing something right." Shamir had a job as a telemarketer, something Elvis did once for about a month, reminding people they owed bills, as if they didn't know it, before he got the job at the home. John had a kid with his girlfriend and worked as a supervisor at a food caterer. He was doing well. Delto was older, at least thirty. He was the husband of John's sister and had three kids. Delto lived in Yonkers, but John's mom was in Elvis's neighborhood, so he saw him frequently. "At five or six, we get in front of the building. If it's a weekend, we have a couple of beers. If someone has a car, we'll cruise around, get something to eat, just chill. Gary lives nearby, and Shamir lives two buildings away. I met them from working the truck. We're not friends anymore. We're family."

"It's important to have friends you can depend on," Ms. Oliver said.

She thought this over, this almost tribal rite he had enacted with his buddies, and it was fascinating to her but also a little unnerving. In her long life, she had never had to obsess over survival in the way he had, worry about such depravity around her. She was doing her best to counsel him, but sometimes the task seemed to enlarge beyond one old woman's power. Other people, most people, they found no need to tattoo closeness into their skin. There were times, when she went into the darker reaches of her imagination, that she felt as if she were navigating through clouds.

Elvis said, "You better believe it's very important for me to have friends. I've always been criticized all my life. In the Dominican Republic, we were the worst kids in the neighborhood. Complaints would come in to my grandmother. A lot weren't true; a lot were. Like once I got taken down to the precinct because someone had scratched *Elvis* into someone's car. It turned out it was this other kid, who was a mute and his name was Elvis, too. I was home all day playing marbles. In the truck, I was always told by my mother and stepfather that I wasn't doing something right. In school, I was stressed out, and teachers were always telling me I wasn't a good student. I didn't think that was true. I thought I was smart. The kind of compliments I got were, 'You better get a seventy-five, or I'll whip your ass.' Then in high school, letters would come home that I didn't attend this or that. And now you're walking down the street, and people see your baggy jeans and think you're a fucking criminal. I've always been judged in certain ways wherever I've gone. I've felt that I've been criticized most of my life. And mostly unjustly criticized. People look at me, and I'm reading a big thick book on the train, but they see my baggy jeans and my tattoos and they make their judgment—this is a criminal. But the residents in the home have accepted me. You accepted me right away.

You saw me as I really am. With the residents' relatives, it's different. It's happened to me a few times. I would get into an elevator with relatives who were visiting. I'd say, 'Hello, how are you?' Very polite, a smile on my face. No response. Eyes on the floor. Okay. They're reacting to my baggy clothes, my tattoos. Then I'll get out on the same floor and walk into the room where their parent is, and the person will say, 'Oh, this is the wonderful young man who has been so helpful to me, takes me to the service every week, gets me my cookies.' Then they're all nice and warm and cuddly. Well, a little late, guys! In the elevator a minute ago, you wouldn't acknowledge I even existed."

She looked at him, alarmed. "Oh, Elvis, it's so different with other people. My great-grandson goes to swimming. His parents pay two hundred dollars for him to go to Tai-chi. They rent the Y to have a swimming party. These kids are living it up. And people in other countries are living in such poverty and malnutrition. I never realized how awful it was until I heard about your life. In school they should teach kids how to live a meaningful life and how to relate to other people. You have kids shooting up principals and teachers, and you have teachers abusing kids. What are they thinking? Where does this come from?"

"Kids today make their lives a living hell, Miss Oliver, and parents contribute to that. They buy them all this expensive clothing. They don't even know what it is. Then they get older, and their parents can't do it anymore. And so they turn to crack to pay for it. They spend more time on their looks than their studies."

He, of course, would shortly be a father, and he seemed to be rehearsing his own parental intentions, figuring out with her how he was going to do it.

Across the pond from them was a woman in a wheelchair, and a friend was taking movie pictures of her.

Ms. Oliver said, "Sometimes I'm here, and I feel I'm from another place."

"I understand you completely. This resident I work with says he hates it here because it's a death house. He feels everyone else is a deadbeat waiting to die. And he's a fighter. He was saying, 'I want to do things. I want to go out. I want to drink. I want to have sex. Maybe I should call an escort.' He said one of the other guys here did that. He had someone take him to a hotel, and they had an escort come. I heard that too, but I don't believe it. I think he said that to the guy just to gas him up."

"Elvis, there's a bug on my neck."

He brushed it off.

She said, "Elvis, what is a DVD movie?"

"It's a movie on a disk instead of a videocassette tape. It's read by a laser, and you can see it on a TV."

"Oh my goodness. All this is above me."

Dusk setting in, he took her to dinner. They saw one of the other residents there, who sarcastically liked to call the dining room "the Garden of Eden," and so now he said, "Welcome to the Garden of Eden." Elvis had to move the woman who sat next to Ms. Oliver out of the way. That didn't sit well with her. She snapped at him, "Get your hands off. I didn't tell you what to take. I didn't go to school for nothing. What college did you go to?"

"I didn't go yet."

"I went to the best."

"Home schooling?"

"Yeah, right, big shot."

· *16* ·

He got off the subway at Saint Nicholas and 181st Street and came out into the day. A knot of listless kids was loitering around the exit. "Welcome to the future of our neighborhood," Elvis thought.

He walked down 180th Street, which he usually avoided, because that was where his mom's food truck was parked for years, directly across from the post office. Even seeing the spot brought back piercing memories he had no interest in revisiting. Wind took garbage into the air, blew it past him. Along the street was an alley, and deep in the alley was the little homemade basketball court where he first met Gary, John, and Shamir.

Across the street, he noticed a homeless guy dragging a cast-off couch down the street, working against the weight of the thing, the cumbersome shape. "I've seen that guy for years," he said. "Always homeless. I don't know how he hangs on."

He passed a weedy little kid he knew, and bummed a candy off him.

A young woman walked by, complete stranger, jewelry clanging on her. She took Elvis in with her eyes and said, "You're handsome," and kept walking.

Elvis smiled to himself. He said, "Now I'm gassed up all day."

He saw his mother the other day. He didn't see her much, even though she lived a couple of blocks away. He had never fully forgiven her for leaving him alone when he was fifteen. He found out she was casting around for work, looking to babysit or clean apartments. "I really don't like my mom doing that sort of thing," he said. "She still has pins and needles from carpal tunnel syndrome, even though she had operations on both wrists. I mean, nobody wants their mom scrubbing floors."

He was annoyed about last night, another roach issue. "This man who lives with me gives me this Dominican drink. I'm enjoying the drink. I put it on the dresser and go to the bathroom, and I come back and there's a roach in it. I can't put anything on the dresser. In the bathtub last week, there was a water bug. A big one. Who needs a water bug in their bathtub? And nothing works. The bathroom door doesn't close. Place is a joke."

Frowning to himself, he kept walking, hands jammed into the pockets of his jeans, and nodded at a window high up in a building. That's where a friend lived with his mother, and when times where bad for Elvis after his mother left, there was always a plate with a hot meal there for him.

He peeked into his brother's barbershop, wanting to take a cut. No sign of Ronny. He had been talking with him about going to the Dominican Republic to visit their grandmother, maybe their mother going, too, but the fares they checked on the Internet were too steep, no way they could afford it.

He pushed into Villalegre for lunch. He slid into the next-to-last booth. The paneling there was loose and squeaked when you leaned against it. Elvis used to think the noise was rats scurrying about. He ordered a steak sandwich, cooked rare, onions on it.

A strapping guy came in, dressed in workout clothes, and squatted on a stool near Elvis. He had Popeye muscles. They acknowledged each other. Elvis hadn't seen him in a while.

"What up?" Elvis said.

"You still working?" he asked Elvis.

"Yeah."

"Keeps you honest."

"That's right."

The guy used to buy chimis from the truck, sometimes gave Elvis a hard time, beat him up now and then. That was long ago, forgotten conflict.

The waiter came with the food and laid out the silverware and napkin. Elvis took a bite out of his steak sandwich and asked the guy on the stool, "What you doing now?"

The man hesitated a moment, looked like someone had just punched him, crumpled a napkin in his fist, then said, "Working for the city."

Elvis nodded, not knowing what that meant, then asked, "You with that same girl?"

"Yeah, we're expecting."

"Well, congratulations."

"Thanks."

"Boy or girl?" Elvis asked.

"We don't know," the man said. "Going to be surprised."

"I had a friend, the doctors said it was a girl. They checked it four times. They got all these things for a shower, girl stuff. The baby came out. It was a boy."

The guy laughed.

Elvis said nothing about expecting himself, not a word. He didn't feel comfortable spreading the word. It was different. Not only was he unmarried, not all that remarkable in his circles, but the woman was not someone he felt close to, might ever sleep with again.

"So what you doing for the city?" Elvis said.

The man looked the other way and mumbled, "NYPD."

Elvis said, "Oh, I notice how you took your time to tell me you're a cop."

"Yeah, well." The man concentrated on his grilled cheese.

Elvis didn't want to say anything that would be hurtful to the man's pride, so he said nothing. Bury the thought. After a moment, Elvis shrugged and said, "You got to do what you got to do."

The meaning of that wasn't lost on Elvis. If you were from the hood and you became a cop, you were looked on as a sellout. To become a cop and still live in the hood, well, that didn't happen every day. So you did what this guy did. You didn't advertise your profession. You closed your eyes to some of the things you saw. You watched your back. But Elvis understood how his old pal could do it. You just had to gaze at his biceps.

Elvis had his own well-motivated distrust of the cops. He had seen a lot of harassment. You're driving a nice car, they pull you over automatically. Tell you to clear the corner. One day when Elvis was about twelve, a cop smacked him against a supermarket on 186th Street. A cop was putting a ticket on a car. Elvis was walking with his friend and said, as a joke, "Oh, look, they're giving me a ticket again." The cop signaled to him, "C'mon here." He shoved Elvis against the gate and smacked him in the head. Elvis went to the precinct and wanted to sign a complaint and was told it had to be filled out in pen. He asked to borrow a pen. They said no—there were no pens there.

"Once the cops came out of a minivan, and I had a Jimmy Jazz bag," was a story he liked to tell. "I had just bought some pants. They searched my Jimmy Jazz bag. They said I had come out of a drug building. They embarrassed me in front of my neighbors. If they see baggy jeans or baggy shirts or a fitted hat, they stop you; they think you're trouble."

At Villalegre, Elvis and the cop chatted idly about women, how the man's wife had eighty pairs of shoes, turned over her wardrobe every season. Go figure.

Elvis said, "The more I hear this stuff, the further I get away from marriage."

"Yeah, I hear you, but there're kids."

"Yeah, they're a blessing."

Elvis hoped so. Blessing or burden, he would find out firsthand.

His stomach full, Elvis left as two new customers pushed through the door. He went to All Star Barbershop to take a cut. The guy there did Ronny's hair, and Elvis used the place as his backup when Ronny wasn't around. The shop also specialized in tattoos and piercing. Rap music blared from the speakers. On the walls hung photographs of Dominican major league baseball players: Sammy Sosa, Pedro Martinez, Alex Rodriguez. Two shifty-eyed guys were playing checkers on the window seat, moving the pieces without saying anything.

Elvis scooped up a copy of *Sucesos*, flipped through the usual run of grisly deaths, put it down. "I always say, if I had to live my life over, I wouldn't change a thing," he mused to some barbershop companions. "I know that sounds weird, but it's the way I feel. All the things I did and what happened to me, they made me a stronger person and a more apprecia-tive person. I used to think I was just saying that. But I sat down and thought about it. It would have been nice if it was easier, but I believe in fate. A lot of people who have had it easy don't make anything of their life. My friend Gary, I'm getting a little worried about him, the road he's moving on now. He just had a baby. He's nineteen. He had it too easy. Now all he's thinking about is money, money. He works in a dress factory. His girlfriend, she's twenty. She doesn't work. He was always saying to me, 'Why are you volunteering at a place where you get nothing?' I told him, 'You'll see.' He's going nowhere. He's kind of a vain guy. He'll be in someone else's car, and he'll act like it's his car. He knows how to drive, but he doesn't know how to earn money to buy a car. His mother spoiled him. Gave him things even though she didn't have many things. He always had the best sneakers, the best haircuts. He got too much too soon is the way I see it. That hasn't been me. There's nothing good that I've had too soon."

After getting his cut, looking good, he went and sat down on a pyramid-shaped stoop next to his building to chill. Sometimes he got ideas here for his rhymes. It was uncomfortable, perching on a pointed tip, and the sidewalk reeked of detritus, but Elvis liked it. He was accustomed to it. He had been sitting on this spot for years and was beholden to routine. Pretty much every day after work, he came here and sat, suffused in the rhythms and clatter of the street. His friends would eventually wander by.

It was how you hooked up with Elvis; you just looked for him at his usual spots. Otherwise, he was difficult to reach.

He had no e-mail, no cell phone, none of the conventional appendages of modern life. "I don't like cell phones," he said. "Easy way to reach me. Be bothered. I'm a loner. People call on the phone, and they have nothing to say. Talking just to yap. Talking just to hear their voice."

Once, a year or so ago, he had a cell phone and lost it. Some girls took sick on the street when Elvis and a friend were passing by. They helped get the girls to a hospital, and in the confusion he lost his phone. He didn't miss it and so never bothered to replace it.

It was hot, even as the afternoon sun slouched lower in the sky, and it contributed to a feeling of listlessness. There was barely a trace of a breeze. Odors from piles of garbage bags at the curb wafted through the still air. The streets were crowded with parked cars, even in front of the fire hydrants, the sidewalks full of idle men and women, wearing boredom and carrying the weight of their sorrows, shuffling along to indeterminate destinations, to nowhere.

A stray dog wandered up to him, nuzzled his foot. It had one of those pathetic looks dogs have when they're short a meal and think you can help them out. Elvis shooed it away, and it trotted off.

He yawned, looked up and down the street. "In a lot of ways this neighborhood is like my old neighborhood in the Dominican Republic. Same people, same situations, same gossip. People get into other people's lives. They mess up relationships. They talk just to talk. They're bored, and they have nothing to do."

Shamir's younger brother appeared, playing.

"Your brother around?" Elvis asked.

"Yeah, he's upstairs."

Elvis went over to Shamir's apartment. He was taking a shower, while his girlfriend watched a TV soap in their bedroom. Shamir was nineteen and had dropped out of high school. Shamir's parents, done with their day's work selling shirts on the street, were slouched on the couch in the tiny, cramped living room, looking at a Spanish talk show with Shamir's grandmother, the chatter self-conscious in the dim light.

The show was *Laura en America*, a Jerry Springer looka-like show taped in Peru and broadcast in the United States on Telemundo every weekday at four in the afternoon. People in the neighborhood established their schedules around the show, centering their lives on its juicy revelations. Shamir's parents filled Elvis in on essential information for him to understand what was happening. It seemed that Laura Bozzo, the host of the show, had been under house arrest for months and been forced to sleep at the studio. She had been accused of receiving more than three million dollars in laundered money from the country's former intelligence chief, who was on trial for corruption. She maintained that he was blackmailing her. None of these nasty inconveniences seemed to have dampened her enthusiasm for her guests. The guests were the usual daytime fare, couples locked in domestic combat, ready to murder each other or at least bash each other's brains in. One guy had to be kept restrained. Another was hustled off the set by two brutish security guards.

"There's no Spanish person who hasn't seen this show," Elvis said, watching it with a certain bemusement, following a little of it, glancing out the window from time to time.

Some black-and-white footage was shown of a guy selling drugs, caught on a hidden camera. And there was the guy sitting in one of the guest chairs.

Ads came on for phone cards to call Mexico, for Thermo shorts that caused you to sweat off weight.

"Man, what's that about?" Elvis said. "That's some weird way to lose weight." He ached, too much lifting at the home, and he kneaded the back of his neck.

Uninterested in the television badinage, Shamir shrugged into some baggy clothes, and he and Elvis went outside to sit on the stoop. Shamir only hung for a short while, because he was supposed to report to his telemarketing job for a few hours. "Catch you later," he told Elvis.

"Catch you later."

Elvis's eyes roved over the assortment of women that passed by his spot on the block, searching for ones worth a second look. Two women sauntered by, looking insolent and cool, wearing the tightest imaginable shorts. "All you see are pretty girls with no brains," Elvis said flatly. "I know those girls. Anytime you see girls chilling with guys on the corner, it's not good. It's not a good investment."

Cars flashed past. A scruffy guy with dented cheeks came by, selling batteries. Elvis bought two for a couple of dollars for Ms. Oliver's remote control, which had been on the blink.

Elvis noticed a couple down the block and took them in with cold appraisal. "See, here's one reason I'm afraid to get married. The guy who owns that store, he's been married for years, got kids, and one day he finds his wife in bed with another man, in his bed. And she knew he was coming and did it deliberately. I don't know what's wrong with him, but they're still together. I see a lot of deceit. I don't know who to trust."

Juan Martinez came by, Elvis's best friend. They grew up together, went to school together. Elvis felt he was one of the few people he could have an intelligent conversation with.

"What's up?" Elvis said

"Got some CDs," Juan said. He was twenty-one. He was going to plumbing school and doing some practicing. He lived with his father. He didn't have one yet, but he planned to get a unity tattoo too, become an official member of the brotherhood.

Juan hung for a short while, took in the scene. Elvis said, "We used to play basketball a lot, and we argued all the time about who was winning, who was better."

"No argument, I was better," Juan said. "Not any question."

"What're you doing out of work?" Elvis asked.

"I'm done."

"Okay, if you say so."

"I can't hang anymore. I got to go get some plantains."

A guy passed by and nodded hello to Elvis. Not long ago, Elvis had lost his keys. The guy appeared and was clutching keys in his hands. Elvis asked if he could look at those keys; he had just lost his. The man was reluctant. He was suspicious. Elvis told him to just hold them up, let him take a look. The guy shoved Elvis, and Elvis punched him and sent him reeling across the sidewalk. The guy continued to say hello to Elvis. Strife, always strife, on the streets.

Elvis looked up and down the street, some listless panhandlers with glassy-dark eyes, some guys in grungy jeans torn at the knees, one of them belching loudly, some worn-out mothers wheeling home plump bags of groceries. Drug dealers liked to use the mothers to conceal drugs in their baskets, move them stealthily around the neighborhood. Nothing of interest. He sat a few more minutes and then decided to go upstairs, through the paint-chipped hallways. He wanted to tidy up and maybe catch a cartoon, end the day on a light note.

· *17* ·

Today was different: Ms. Oliver was down in the dumps.

Just the other day, her daughter Janet had gotten her a new phone, outfitted with those oversized buttons best suited for her inaccurate fingers. She hadn't even used it yet, it was charging, and someone stole it when she was out of the room for an hour, tops. She had also had a plastic cup, a souvenir from a Spanish party, stolen along with a basket and a pair of pink slippers. Someone else had had perfume stolen. A man had had a pair of new socks swiped from his dresser. Hard to believe. What wouldn't people steal?

Elvis was mad, really mad. He couldn't stand it when someone took advantage of Ms. Oliver, a defenseless woman in a wheelchair, her eyes so bad, she sometimes didn't know things were gone until someone else pointed it out.

She was shaken and dazed, and feeling a little twitchy.

There was that whine behind her eyes and the throb in her temples. She said, "It's really bothering me. You know I didn't sleep well last night. I usually sleep a good eight hours, and I didn't last night. I'm wondering if I should put those pictures of the family away."

He frowned. "No, c'mon. You shouldn't have to worry about your family pictures. You shouldn't have to worry about none of your stuff."

He said that a guy in a nearby room, someone had swiped his singing fish off the wall, a battery-operated thing that, when you pressed it, played songs like "Don't Worry. Be Happy."

"Elvis, check to see if my banana is there."

"I hid it in the basket on the window."

"Imagine, we have to hide my banana."

"The banana's here. Your fruit is intact. Don't worry, this is going to be all right."

Many people wandered in and out of the home, and a certain number of them had sticky fingers. Ms. Oliver knew this, and so did the other residents. They often lamented their losses. Who knew who was to blame? Truth and rumor swept through the home like air from the air-conditioning.

The culprits never seemed to get caught, though Ms. Oliver suspected the many "floaters" who materialized one day and then quickly evaporated, sometimes never to be seen again. One of them had been particularly curious about the workings of one of the phones. Security's belated response was to put a chain on her replacement phone and bolt it to the wall—as if she was living in a public housing project in the Bronx or a prison cell—and to program the phone so that it would ring if it was removed from the room.

She really needed cheering up, to wash this bitter taste from her mouth. Elvis let her know that if a bunch of bad things happened to her all at once, then next week was bound to be better. Come to think of it, there had been a bunch. The other morning her roommate blocked her path to the bathroom, and when she went to lunch one of the women at her table really gave it to her, making her skin prickle: "Oh you dropped something. You're so sloppy." She started crying.

See that, he told her, you're overdue for some good happenings.

They went down to the garden, and Elvis opened a letter from her daughter Joyce, with the latest jokes from the Internet. This time it was a list of funny signs.

Elvis read them out: "On a septic tank truck: We're number one in the number two business.

"On a proctologist's door: To expedite your visit, please back in.

"On a plumber's truck: We repair what your husband fixed.

"On an optometrist's door: If you don't see what you're looking for, you've come to the right place.

"On a fence: Salesmen welcome. Dog food is expensive.

"On a car dealership: The best way to get back on your feet? Miss a car payment.

"At a funeral home: Drive carefully, we can wait."

They laughed and laughed. Even when some of the lines weren't all that funny, they couldn't contain themselves, Ms. Oliver metamorphosing before him, becoming replenished through a comic bandage.

Filled with happiness, she said, "I needed that. I haven't laughed in days; all these things going wrong."

Elvis said, "I've got a joke. There's this businessman. He wants to get a loan from a banker for an operation to save his life. He goes to this stingy, stingy banker and says he needs a loan and explains it's for this operation. The banker says he can't help him because the guy has no credit. The guy tells him that he is the most coldhearted person he has ever met. The banker says, 'That really hurts, calling me that. I'll tell you what. I have a glass eye. If you can tell me which one it is, I'll give you the loan.' 'That's easy,' the guy says, 'it's your left one. The banker says, 'How did you know that? No one has ever guessed it.' The guy says, 'Because I saw a glimmer of sympathy in it, so I knew it had to be the glass one.'"

"Elvis, you've cheered me up. I've been feeling glum lately. Like I don't belong anywhere. Like when you're in your home, you feel you belong. Lately I haven't felt I belonged. And I have to spend the rest of my life here."

"Now don't feel that way. Of course you belong. You could belong anywhere."

Easy for the young to say such things, she knew that. How easy it was.

School had started at Long Island University, which cut into his time at the home, though he still managed to do his work in the religious services department and put in some hours with the man he helped with his physical therapy. He wasn't able to spend as much time with Ms. Oliver, but he found his way to her room a couple of times most weeks. He refused to take any more money from her, no longer felt comfortable about that; she was his friend. She wished he would, for she had money and he didn't, but he was insistent. Elvis was enjoying college. The first day he went to Brooklyn to register, putting on a jacket and tie and pants that didn't hang below his waist, everyone treated him with such respect that he was glowing about the experience for weeks. He had never imagined he would go to a place like Long Island University with a real campus and well-scrubbed modern classrooms, students earnestly drifting from class to class. He told Ms. Oliver that he found the work stimulating; there had been a discussion about democracy in history class, and he had to write a three-page essay on the subject.

He said, "I'm writing how I wasn't sure what democracy was when I was picked out of a crowd by a cop and when I asked why I was picked, I was shoved against the fence."

"You know, you haven't lived through the McCarthy period. The government ruined people's careers and lives by forcing them to tell on other people."

"I need to have someone explain to me what democracy is. Because I haven't seen too much of it."

"I know how you feel."

"When I'm doing my schoolwork, I've found I've got to be careful. I haven't done homework in a while, and I found when I was writing something for school I was using my slang, which is what I use when I write my rap lyrics. Like instead of writing *the* as *t-h-e,* I wrote *d-a.* I've got to watch that."

"Yes, you had better. Elvis, I wanted to ask you, growing up, if your mother didn't speak English, who helped you with your homework?"

"No one did. We had a TV set with three channels. One was a Spanish channel with all inane stuff, soap operas and all. So I tuned it to thirteen and twenty-one. I watched cartoons until three, and at four *Sesame Street* was on. I learned the alphabet and things from that show."

"So Big Bird taught you English?"

"Well, he sure helped a lot. That's one smart bird."

"Not a birdbrain, huh? Speaking of school, did you have much Shakespeare in high school?"

"Come to think of it, we didn't. We had some. I remember we were studying *Hamlet* and the Clinton scandal happened, and we forgot *Hamlet* and started talking about that in English class."

Elvis went on to talk about his college speech class. "The other day, I was supposed to do a talk, and I was going to do a rap song I was working on, but I didn't know if that would go over well. I was breaking my head trying to think about something to say. So I bought a pack of gum, and I was chewing away in class, and I asked the question 'How many of you have contributed to your country?' Nobody raised their hand. And I saw a lot of people chewing gum, and I asked, 'What did you do with your wrapper? Probably threw it away. What you need to do is keep the tinfoil to wrap the gum in.' Then I demonstrated. I chewed half a stick of gum and then wrapped it up. That was my demonstration of how to contribute to the community and keep it clean. The class was cracking up."

"Well, that was quick thinking, Elvis."

Changing the subject, Elvis asked, "I was wondering, Do you think terrorism is a form of protest?"

"Yes, because terrorists think they're right."

"But what drives them? It just can't be the religion. They have to be brainwashed."

"Because they believe they'll go to a better place."

"But someone has to brainwash you."

"Yes, their leaders."

"Socrates believed that in a healthy man every organ is united in his body and working together like an orchestra," Elvis said. "If you were to see the world we're living in now, everything is not united. This is not a healthy man. There is always someone power hungry."

"Well, the country is going down the drain. After every election, all you hear is the Republicans and the Democrats fighting with each other. They never work together. They're so divided."

"It's sad."

"Money, power, greed. Too many greedy people. I've always remembered the quote 'to thine own self be true.' I've never been guided by what someone else told me. And I've lived like that. And you are that way, too."

"Yes, I am. Would you like some ginger ale?"

"I certainly would.

"You know, Elvis, I dreamed last night about O. J. Simpson. There was this story about him on the front page of the *Wall Street Journal*. And he was a lawyer. I don't know what that was about."

"Maybe you were thinking about your phone getting stolen, and you hired him to represent you."

"Maybe that was it."

They talked about Internet dating sites, a new phenomenon that she had just learned about on one of the talk shows, and Ms. Oliver said she knew someone who met a man that way. "I think that's a scary way to meet someone, isn't it?" she said.

Elvis said, "This guy who volunteers here, his cousin went on a dating site, and he met this woman and she sounded good. They sent each other pictures of themselves. She sent this picture, and she was just gorgeous. So he arranged to meet her. She was nothing like the picture. She was chunky and missing a tooth."

"I don't understand all of that. You know, they used to say, 'Beauty is only skin deep.'"

"Miss Oliver, I'm going to tell the last joke of the day. There are these three good friends on a cruise. Something happens, and there's a shipwreck. Most everyone survives. The three friends are on a raft together on the sea. One of them sees this old, old bottle floating by. He grabs it and rubs it. A genie appears, and he says he has three wishes to grant them. The first friend says, 'Okay, I'm twenty-five years old. I have a beautiful apartment and one year more of college, but I want to go back to my old life when I had all these girlfriends. I want my old life back.' So the genie sends him back to his old life. The second friend says, 'I've been married twelve years and I've got kids, but I miss my old single life; I want to go back to that,' so the genie sends him back. Now it's the third friend's turn. He thinks and thinks, and then he says, 'You know, I'm bored. I wish my friends were back.'"

A woman who had heard about Elvis and Ms. Oliver and their relationship had sent them a book that made her think warmly of them. It had been a particular favorite of hers as a child. It was called *Wilfrid Gordon McDonald Partridge* by Mem Fox. Sitting in the garden under the tranquilizing sun, Elvis read it to her. It was about a young boy by that name who lived beside a retirement home. His favorite old person was Nancy Alison Delacourt Cooper, and he liked her because she had four names like him. Everyone thought she had lost her memory, and Wilfrid didn't even comprehend what memory was, but by accident he helped her find it. The book was about old people, as seen through a small child's eye, and it was refreshingly nonpatronizing. When they finished, they both thought it was sweet, and that the characters were something like them, only younger.

"That was a really lovely story," Ms. Oliver said.

"Boy, it sure was," Elvis said. "They were two people far apart in age who liked each other a lot, and that's just like us."

"Yes. Like us."

He took her to her room and then said he would be going. He reached over, and she gave him a kiss on his cheek. She sometimes did that, when she felt especially close, really happy that he had been there.

· *18* ·

Cool rainy day. Ashen sky. Drops ran down her window.

And then the girls stopped by. That was still how she referred to her twin daughters, even now that they were over seventy. The girls. Joyce took the train in from Westchester, and Janet drove up from her apartment forty blocks south of the home. They were in high spirits, buoyant.

Wide awake, Ms. Oliver swiveled her face from one to the other, proud of what she saw. She leaned back and let their aliveness wash over her.

Janet had on a red dress and pearls. Joyce wore a blue warmup suit. Janet immediately got busy tidying up the room, folding sweaters and stowing away socks. She was a cleaner. Always was.

"Ma, what are all these napkins here?" she said, hoisting a

stack of about a hundred napkins. "What do you need all these napkins for?"

Ms. Oliver studied the napkins and said, "Well, I guess I don't."

"No, you surely don't."

She stuffed them into a bureau drawer.

While Janet tidied, Joyce talked. That was her specialty.

She was always the talker, and Janet had to fight to cram in a word, express herself at all. They were different people; everyone saw that. Joyce was like her father, noisy and bossy, while Janet was like her mother, calm and collected.

Ms. Oliver sat in her wheelchair and looked at them with a glint of fun in her eyes. She always felt good when the girls were there.

They sat and traded memories. There were plenty of them.

Joyce said, "Ma, you were always such a fantastic cook. I think it rubbed off on me. You know, I make tons of candy every season and give it out to everyone."

Janet said, "Joyce was always cooking as a kid. I did the dishes. Joyce was a great cook, but she didn't like to clean up. So we struck a deal. Joyce made me something to eat, and I did the dishes. Dad used to say that I couldn't boil water."

Ms. Oliver, giving an impish look, said, "Your kids still say the same thing."

Janet said, "Hey, Ma! Remember the time when we were small, and it was Christmastime, and we were helping to clean the house? We were like three. We were pulling the sheets out of the hamper and putting them in the bathtub. We said, 'Ma, we're washing clothes.'"

"Oh boy, do I remember that," Ms. Oliver said.

Joyce said, "Remember when Dad brought some rolls and you couldn't find them?"

"Yes, I had told him to bring home some rolls, and I looked everyplace for them," Ms. Oliver said. "I called him at work. He said they were on the table. Finally, I looked under the table, and the two of you were eating them. Each of you had a big roll sticking out of your mouth."

"Were we devils as kids?" Joyce asked.

"Yes, you were."

A nurse arrived to take Ms. Oliver's temperature. Earlier, when Joyce had greated her mother with a hug and a kiss, she thought her face felt warm. Concerned that her mother might have a fever, she called for a nurse to come and check her.

The nurse looked at the thermometer: 98.1. "She's fine," the nurse said.

Joyce said, "I'll bet she normally is 97.6. Because she was hot."

"She's never been wrong," Janet said. "It's hard getting used to."

"I can be wrong once in a while."

"Welcome to the club," Janet said.

"Listen, it's hard being perfect."

Joyce had brought some candy, indulging her mother's sweet tooth, and Ms. Oliver tremulously helped herself to some, and they listened to her stomach struggling to digest the sweets. In the hall, two aides were pestering each other.

Janet began to massage her mother's hand. She was a licensed massage therapist, one of her many talents. She had taught music in high school for thirty-three years in the New York public schools, before retiring. She also was an organist, and she sang in a choir, sometimes performing in Carnegie Hall.

For her part, Joyce had been an actress and model in her youth. She had landed roles on a few soap operas—*As the World Turns, Guiding Light, Search for Tomorrow*. Usually, she was cast as a nurse, though once she got to play a doctor. As a model, she did print ads for the beers and soft drinks. Once Clairol hired her, bleached her hair blond.

Now long retired from acting, she was a psychooncologist. She saw patients at her home and did work with women with breast cancer in Aruba four times a year. "My real love is terminally ill people," she would tell people. "I love it. I love it." Death and its mysteries didn't scare or depress her. "Dying, schmying, it happens to everyone," she liked to say. "I've got a good attitude about dying. I have no problem with death and dying. I have no fear about it. There are emotions but no fear."

Joyce told her mother about one of her cases: "This woman, she had cancer, and all her life she had been a doormat. Walk over me. Walk over me. More than anything, she wanted to be in charge. And she wanted to be a dancer. So I did drama therapy with her. I made her the dance teacher, and I played the klutzy student. And she loved it. It gave her happiness."

Ms. Oliver said, "You know, when you two were teenagers, I worried about keeping you out of trouble. I read an article that said keep them busy, and so I did. But maybe I kept you too busy. Here you are seventy, and you're busy, busy, busy."

Janet said nothing. She was working on her mother's legs and feet.

Ms. Oliver said, "You know, I loved taking the grandkids places. I miss it."

A few minutes went by. Joyce spoke up: "Ma, how do you stay so beautiful?"

Ms. Oliver said, "A lot of people tell me that."

Joyce said, "Because you are. You don't look a day over eighty."

Ms. Oliver said, "I always say, 'You live the best you can, you eat the best you can, and you'll be all right.'"

They looked at her. She nodded at them.

"Oh, Ma," Joyce said.

"Oh, Ma," Janet said.

· *19* ·

"What mammal lives the longest?"

"Whale."

"Tortoise or turtle."

"Elephant."

"A human."

"Right, a human. Humans live a hundred years, so you have to take that into consideration. You see that right here."

Only about two dozen people were in the room. After all, you had to be lucid to play Trivia Galore, and that prerequisite eliminated most of the home. It was dim out.

In rapid-fire staccato fashion, the host asked the questions, and whoever thought they knew the answer shouted it out.

"What baseball player was walked the most times?"

No one knew it was Babe Ruth. (The answers were a little outdated; Barry Bonds now holds the record.)

"Who claims to be the most recognized person in the world?"

"Muhammad Ali."

"That's absolutely right."

There were several sharp players, always speaking up before you could even think. You had to be swift to beat them.

"What's the world's most popular nonalcoholic beverage?"

"Coffee," Ms. Oliver said.

"Good for you, Ollie." Got one.

"What city is visited mostly by Americans?"

No one knew.

"Tijuana. We go to get our drugs there. Wholesale."

On and on.

"How many holes are there in a ten-pin bowling ball?"

"Three," Ms. Oliver said.

"Got it."

Yes, she wasn't bad, got her licks in here and there.

"Who nominated Richard Nixon for president in 1972?"

"Somebody stupid."

The answer was Spiro Agnew.

"What is the shortest verse in the Bible?"

"'Jesus wept.'"

"Right."

"What does a deltiologist collect?"

Nobody had a clue. "Postcards."

Whew, what a session; you needed to be some sort of genius to answer a few of those questions. Then, when Ms. Oliver got upstairs, Elvis came in with the news, excited. As of 2:14 P.M. Monday, he was the father of a baby girl. He was beaming.

She smiled at him, picking up on his exhilaration. "So how do you feel?" she asked him.

"I really feel good."

She asked the baby's name. Eleny Mercedes, the middle name after his beloved grandmother.

She asked her weight.

Just over seven pounds.

"Does she look like you?"

"Yeah, I think she does."

"Now remember, you have to put all this in the proper perspective," she said with a frown of concern.

"I know. I made a very stupid mistake that I'm proud to say is a blessing. I had this one-night stand. We didn't have any relationship, and there was nothing that could be done, so here we are."

He wasn't going to atone any further, not express regrets. After all, she was the one who had told him to live a life free of regrets. Mistakes happen, life is sown with peril, but you can't redo the past or become craven. You have to take responsibility and move on, and right now he wanted to marvel at having a child. The truth was he was unbelievably happy, and he didn't want to feel any shame in that.

She could see that but didn't want him consumed and sidetracked, off on some dreamer's errand. As if thinking aloud, she said, "Well, Elvis, tell me, do you have warm feelings toward the mother?"

He hesitated, thinking before he answered. She knew how to ask the right questions. He said, "I'm ashamed to say I don't have any feelings at all."

She watched him closely, not wanting to admonish him, just trying to set him on a wise path. "Well, if you don't, you really have to limit your relationship. Because, as they say, hell hath no fury like a woman scorned. You have to see the baby but keep it platonic."

"What's that word?"

"*Platonic*. It means 'don't have sex.' Just talk, okay?"

He stroked his chin. "That's a new word for me. That's a cool word." He gave that big smile of his.

"Glad you like it. But are you listening to what I'm saying?"

He looked her in the eye. "Yeah, I understand. She has feelings for me. But she understands. She knows I have a girlfriend."

His girlfriend, in fact, was the daughter of Espi Jorge-Garcia, the head of the volunteer office. Her name was Yadira, and the relationship had blossomed a few months ago. He had known her for five years—she often hung around the home with her mother—and she was always supportive of him during hard times. In the past, he had been awkward with her; after all, Espi felt so warmly toward him that she referred to him as her other child, and they used to tease each other that they were brother and sister.

"I've liked her for five years," he told Ms. Oliver. "But I was a coward. I didn't know how to let her know about my feelings. I was going to send her some flowers anonymously, but I couldn't get her address."

"Well, I'm glad, but I worry about the child's mother. Make sure you let her know where you stand."

"I do. I even call Yadira in front of her, so she sees the picture pretty clearly."

She liked that touch, sending an unmistakable message. "Okay, but I don't want you proving that old adage that advice to the young is wasted."

"I won't. I'm happy about the baby. It's changed me. All my life the only people who have accepted the love I have to give are my grandmother and you. I feel that the baby will accept all this. She won't reject my love."

"No, she won't. As long as the baby's mother doesn't expect too much from you."

"She can say and do whatever she wants, as long as the baby is not harmed. I will do what's best for me."

"Well, you have to show that you mean business, not just tell her. You know there's an expression, 'If you didn't wear the moccasins, you can't feel the pain.' You can't just tell someone something because after a while they don't hear it. I tell my daughters the food here is greasy, and they think, Oh, that's just Mom complaining. They don't feel it."

"I know, people just deflect things. But, believe me, I show her that I'm not interested, too."

"Well, good. Keep showing it."

Elvis said that a new guy was sleeping in the living room at his apartment; no one knew who he was. He didn't seem to do anything but drink Johnnie Walker Black, always had a bottle of it in his hand.

"Where's he get the money for it?" Ms. Oliver asked.

Elvis said, "He may have won the Dominican lottery. You know, the tickets are sold illegally here in grocery stores. What happens is the lottery numbers come out in the Dominican Republic. Then they come here like an hour later. So people get the numbers in the Dominican Republic, then call someone here with the numbers and they win. One guy I know won thirty thousand dollars. My friend and I tried it once, but it didn't work. For some reason, we had the wrong numbers—I still don't know why—so we didn't fool with it again."

Ms. Oliver said she had seen something disturbing on TV: "This woman got out of her car at the gas station, and apparently the rubbing against her dress got static electricity on her. When she started filling the tank, a spark came out and ignited, and the car burned up. Did you ever hear of this?"

"That's like self-immolation."

"Well, sort of. She didn't do it on purpose."

Elvis had also seen something disturbing: "I saw a picture of this guy on a Web site called rotten.com who had lost the bottom of his face from the bottom of his eyelids down. He had hit a side rail on a highway on a motorcycle. He was still alive, and then he died."

"Here's another one," Ms. Oliver said. "A girl dropped a pencil in school, and when she reached down to pick it up, it stuck in her. The teacher didn't pull it out because she saw the pencil moving. She knew it was in the heart. They took her to the hospital, and she was okay. I saw this on *Montel Williams*."

"Wow, this is like gross-out day between us," Elvis said.

He took her in to eat. She had a tuna sandwich.

"What a nice waiter I have today," she told him. "I'll have to give you a big tip."

The woman sitting across from her had her dress tangled up in her lap. Elvis straightened it out.

"I'll kill you," she said.

"For straightening your dress?"

"Yes, I'll kill you."

Elvis said, "Tough crowd here."

· *20* ·

In her room, propped against the sun-warmed windowsill, catching a breeze from the slightly opened window, Elvis said he wanted to recite one of his rap songs. In a recent burst of creativity, he had composed a lot of rhymes at night, alone in his room. They told the story of his life, its ugly side and his hopes. He wanted her to hear them, see how he expressed his experiences, even if rap music was not her thing, a long ways removed from Bach and Mozart.

He was a little nervous as he got his sheets out, fumbling with them and dropping one of them on the floor. This was a new audience for him, and he wanted the performance to go well. "If you don't understand something, just ask me and I'll explain it," he told her. "Let me know if I use a term you don't know, because I think there will be some."

"Okay, I'll do that," she said. "Don't worry. If it's something you write, I'm sure I'll find it interesting."

"I really want you to understand it, so I can go slow and repeat stuff. You just stop me and let me know."

She nodded, patient. "Okay, Elvis, if I don't get something, I'll tell you. You know me."

"All right, here we go."

He went straight into it, trying to slow it down, let her keep up, giving it everything he had.

> *Ma I can't feel sorry for you*
> *cause a man done beat you . . . You'se*
> *a grown woman you should know you*
> *train people to treat you/*
> *Don't sit at home waitin for dis*
> *man to feed you . . . you got's to hold*
> *your head up. Do your thang make 'em*
> *need you/*
> *See a lot of ladies feel like Dey ain't*
> *worth a nickel . . . cause a man put 'em*
> *down too much. Da same old ritual*
> *I believe you feel your bah up with*
> *As much as you can carry . . . Don't fuck 'em*
> *Da same day you met 'em. Don expect to*
> *get married/*
> *Worst den a mistake in life is trying*
> *to explain it . . . But den again life is a*

chain of mistakes though, ain't it?
You jump out puddle then try to run
Just to find yourself landing straight
Into a bigger one/
I know . . . I grew up with no socks
no sneaks mad poor son . . . smoked weed
cause bad temper is werst than bad
fortune/
Substituted juice with cold wata
And suga . . . Dere were a lot nights
Wen I had to count o my Rutga/
To keep me company . . . wen I was
Trying to get rid of this ects and
weed . . . to put some motherfucking
food in my stomach/
see not too many people in my life treated
me kindly . . . no father figure had a little
nigga living life blindly/

He came to a line, "spraying is as easy as praying," and guessing she would be stumped by it, stopped to translate. "In my neighborhood, if you bump into someone, they'll shoot you. That's spraying. So I say spraying is as easy as praying. You understand that?"

"Yes. You thought that all up yourself?"

"Yes."

She grew pensive. "That's very good."

"Thank you."

"I was wondering, what's a Rutga?"

"That's a gun popular in the hood. A little too popular."

"I see."

He went on, talking about his grandmother, talking about "time heals all wounds, but time wounds all heels," about "pop a wheelie."

More translation. He said, "You know what I mean by 'pop a wheelie' on a bicycle?"

She shrugged. "No, I can't say I've ever heard that."

"When you pop a wheelie, that means you pull the front wheel up and ride with the back wheel. That's like a fancy move. I had to pop a wheelie because there was no front wheel on my bike."

"Why was there no wheel?"

"I found a bike, and it didn't have a front wheel, and we were too poor to buy a wheel. So I had to always pop a wheelie. It was actually easier to pop a wheelie without a front wheel."

Then he said, "You see how I talked before about the people who stabbed me in the back?"

"Elvis, is that why when you buy something for someone, you never want to take the money?"

"I guess it is."

"Well, you should. If you're getting something for someone, you should take the money. You're entitled to it. If it's someone who can afford it, you should."

"I'm afraid they'll mistake my kindness for weakness."

"Not at all. They say self-preservation is the first law of nature."

"Who said that?"

"I don't know who said that. I've told you this before. And it's true. It's like that plane that crashed in the Andes, and the survivors ate human flesh. Now would we ever think we would eat human flesh and become cannibals? So no one knows what someone will do under what circumstances, says I, Miss Philosopher."

"Your words are very important to me."

"Well, it pleases me if they are."

She was flattered that Elvis wanted to share his rap lyrics with her, stupefying as some of his street talk was to her, and it was quite true that she was not likely to push him to bring in some more of his songs, become a hip-hop devotee at this advanced stage of her life. But this was nice, as if a new moment had been sealed between them, and when you had been around as long as she had and was in this cloistered setting, there was no dismissing something new.

Thinking about these expressions she had never encountered before, the next generation talking, Ms. Oliver said, "You know years ago some young people were executed for using their own language. They were considered witches."

"You're talking way back?"

"Yeah, way back. They say each generation is smarter than the past generation."

"That's because they copy the previous one and add on."

"Until they figure out how to stop fighting, they're not smarter."

"How about some Chunky and ginger ale, Miss Oliver?"

"You've read my mind."

Elvis said he had weird psychic powers: "I'll be walking down the street, and every time I think of a song, my friend starts singing it. All my friends know this about me. The other day I was on the subway, and I told my friend I'm going to write this song down and you'll be singing it when we get off. So we got off, and he started singing. I showed him the paper. That was the song."

"That's like me and my psychic events."

"Maybe we need to open a business together, tell people their futures. We'd sure open some eyes."

"So how's your girlfriend?"

"She's fine. She's doing good."

"You don't have much time to see her."

"But the good thing is she only lives a block away. So it's easy for me to see her."

They talked about UFOs and Bigfoot, and how neither of them believed in them.

It was getting late. He scuffed his shoes together as he studied her menu, looking for her hot dog, looking for her fish cutlet, looking for her grilled cheese.

Elvis said, "Oh, I wanted to tell you something about tea. I saw this on TV. That people boil tea for a certain amount of time, but you really need to boil it for hours to get the real taste. I know you like tea every day, so I wanted you to know that."

"Oh, really? Now you're telling me something I didn't know. I doubt that the home will devote hours to boiling my tea, though."

"Yeah, you got that right. But it's still good to know."

He paused, as another thought came to mind. "I love *The Simpsons*," he said.

"You know, men always like cartoons. When I used to go on dates to the movies, they used to show cartoons, and I found the men always liked those the best."

"It's a getaway. It's an escape. Everybody needs some escape, or they'll go nuts. The cartoon I really like is *Dragon Ball Z*. It's a Japanese cartoon."

"Never heard of it. I'm just not a cartoon person."

He nodded. Gouts of rain began spitting down.

"So you liked my rapping?" he asked her, looking for her seal of approval on his form of music.

She flicked her eyes over him. "Yes, I did, Elvis," she said. "You really told it straight. It has the ring of truth. It was fine."

"Yeah, well, I'm glad you liked it."

"Absolutely."

"Maybe I'll rap to you some more, maybe rap about you."

"Okay, I guess," she said, "rap about me."

It was a good time for them to stop for the day.

· *21* ·

Elvis found his friend Oliver Lora doing some errands for a resident, and they tumbled out the front door of the home and headed uptown to visit the baby and have some dinner. They dropped into the subway, catching the local. They checked out the ads on the wall, selling foot care and zit removal, and the anonymous faces, staring flatly at newspapers or nothing at all. Across from them, a teenage boy was nuzzling his girlfriend, who squealed and looked at him. Elvis and Oliver rubbed away the time with chatter about their days.

When they entered the apartment, it was already crowded, a configuration of men, women, children. What was the deal here? A normal evening. There was always the hectic feel of an open house, people coming and going, never a clear count of who was on hand. It was a jolly group.

The apartment was tidy—nondescript furniture, one window that afforded little light, and no view.

Elvis greeted the baby, giving her a kiss and telling her, "I love you." He called her his "little bubble gum," because she was so pink. "I think she knows my voice," he said, and he tickled her stomach and made some goofy faces at her. He asked the mother how she was, and plopped down on the sofa. He felt weary. His back had been bothering him still, and his wrists, too, lasting reminders from working the truck

He looked around at the crowd. The baby's grandmother said, "This place is always crowded. Seven conversations going at the same time. Pick which one interests you. Then everyone goes, and it's just me and the kids. Then I won't open the door."

Oliver, in a thinly nervous voice, asked to hold the baby, and he cradled her carefully in his arms for a couple of minutes, then gave her back.

Elvis stared at the baby with riveted awareness. He said to Oliver, "You think she looks like me?"

"Yeah, I guess. Got something of your expression."

"She might change as she grows; that stuff happens."

"Yeah, when I was little I looked like my mother, and now I look more like my father."

"I hear you. A few more years, you might be looking like your mother again."

Elvis's mother was there, too, crumpled into the sofa. She liked to visit the baby as much as she could. Elvis asked her about work. She had recently started a new job, putting labels on boxes at a factory in New Jersey. It was going all right, but just a job, hard on her hands, still never fully recovered from the carpal tunnel. She caught the bus to Jersey at seven each morning right outside Elvis's apartment. If she got there early, she'd whistle up to his window, wanting to say hello, and it was annoying him because he would still be asleep. The other day, though, he was glad. He was down to four dollars in his pocket, and his mother gave him a twenty.

His mother told him she thought she was going through menopause.

Elvis said, "Why are you telling me this? Menopause? Do I need to know you're going through menopause?"

"I don't know if you need to know," she told him.

"Well, I can tell you this, I don't. Let's stick to stuff I need to know."

She was small, stout, her short black hair knotted back. She wore black glasses. She had the void look of being here and yet not being here.

The TV was on, the Spanish news, and now there was a report on the new twenty-dollar bills that were being introduced. "Watch this," Elvis said, "so you don't get jacked." Friends of his had gotten ripped off with counterfeit bills.

Elvis was polite but cool toward the baby's mother. She knew he had found a girlfriend, wasn't happy about it.

It was hot in the apartment. Elvis switched on the ceiling fan, glanced over at the baby.

"She's chillin'," he said. "Look, she's chillin'."

Money was tight, many mouths to feed, but Elvis was resolved to follow Ms. Oliver's counsel and make sure he was okay first. He was going to be careful about how much he contributed.

Elvis's voice grew quiet. He cooed at the baby, and then he handed her back to the mother. They stared at each other and didn't say anything. Oliver kept his leg jiggling.

With parting pleasantries, Elvis said he was going, would probably be by tomorrow or the next day, take it easy.

Elvis walked to Villalegre with Oliver. Down the block there was some shouting, but people didn't get startled by shouting on these streets. Oliver had his earphones on, listening to a new CD by 50 Cent. He gave one plug to Elvis so he could hear, and he nodded, yeah, it was good. The sun was down, the days shortening. On the street they folded into the crowd, the usual clots of idle men, hands jammed in their pockets, and swishing young women on the prowl, a parade of high heels and tinted faces. Not too many people looked in any way legitimate. Guys were watching where you held your wallet. On the corner was a guy in a sequined jacket playing a harmonica. A wind sprang up, rustling jackets and lifting skirts. They ran into some guys Elvis knew, and he gave each of them a pound. One had just gotten laid off from his job and was in limbo; Elvis asked about his prospects, and he just shook his head. Turning the corner onto Audubon Avenue, they ran into Juan, Elvis's best friend, who tagged along. On his cell phone, he was dealing with an earlier emergency. His fifteen-year-old sister was returning from high school with her boyfriend, and a guy who disliked the boyfriend stabbed him in the back just outside the subway stop by his home. He was at the hospital being checked out. Juan didn't think the wound was too bad, but he was worried.

Elvis wanted the details, who did it, what it was over. He knew that in his neighborhood assaults didn't have to be over anything. You could wear the wrong shoelaces and get some of your blood on the streets. Juan told him a bunch of guys had jumped the boyfriend a couple of weeks ago, because he was black and they were Hispanic and didn't care for him. One of them happened to be passing by when the kid came out of the subway, and up and put his knife in him. This was about 3:30 P.M., the streets packed, lots of people seeing what they saw all too often.

"Doesn't make any sense," Juan said. "Didn't do anything."

"He was a good student and all, wasn't he?" Elvis said.

"Yeah, honor roll. He didn't deserve this, I'll say that much."

"It's a cultural thing. It's not racism."

"Yeah, and it's a cycle."

Elvis tried to summon up an image of what that must have been like, and it repulsed him. They cruised over to the subway stop, saw the dried blood on the sidewalk, shook their heads.

Villalegre was pretty empty, just a guy on a stool and two guys in a booth. Nobody was talking. Elvis and Juan took the middle booth. Oliver hung back, finishing a cigarette outside. Elvis asked for a cheeseburger and a Diet Coke. Juan just wanted water. The waiter made a scrawl on his pad and vanished into the kitchen.

Juan gave a bland, hopeful look. He seemed to be suffering an emotional vertigo. He lived with his father, who was separated from his mother. His parents had been hounding him, especially his mother, about working and making some money. "My mother is treating me like a baby," he told Elvis. "She's very offensive. She wants me to be a man, which to her means get a job and give her some money." He shook his head. "My mom basically thinks I'm an ATM machine."

Juan had been working as a plumber—the guy at the restaurant called him the Tidy Bowl Man or Mario, after the Mario Brothers, the bulbous video game plumbers—but he was tired of unclogging drains. Lately, he was debating whether to join the navy or go to college. He didn't know when or how he was going to decide between the two, which move to make to change his life. He figured one day he'd just know. Some things you had to feel.

They talked about the trouble that always seemed to haunt the streets and how to keep it at bay. Elvis, being small, said his technique was to look tough, make it clear he wasn't going to take anything from anyone. Juan said he went to work or school and then straight home, staying off the street. "I'm visible, but I'm invisible," he said. "That simple. You see me, but you don't see me."

"You're like a phantom or something, I guess, working under the radar."

The conversation turned to baseball. The playoffs were in swing, the Yankees going against the cursed Red Sox, which had a lot of Dominican players, and the interest was unusually high in Washington Heights. Oliver said he felt genuinely sorry for the Red Sox, their long drought, and would like them to prevail just once, shake off the Bambino curse, but he couldn't watch the games; it pained him. He had dreamed of the big leagues, was an uncommonly talented pitcher, able to send a fastball at eighty-six or eighty-seven miles an hour when he was eighteen. He went to a tryout for the Cyclones, the Mets minor league team that played in Coney Island, but there was so many players there, maybe five hundred, that they never got through half of the onslaught and he never had his chance. Some of the aspirants were jokes, showing up in jeans, not a prayer of making the team. Another date was set, but Oliver lost it and never bothered. Recently he had messed up his arm, needed to get back in shape. "When you feel you could be out there playing and you're not, you can't watch the games," he said. "You can absolutely not watch the games. You got to watch another sport." Oliver was attending a community college downtown, studying respiratory therapy, betting on that as his career.

They sat there in the emptiness of the restaurant, the man

behind the counter running a rag over the surface. He kept a soft patter going with the guy on the stool. Elvis checked his watch. He had to write an English paper tonight, do it in longhand, get to school tomorrow and then the home.

He told Juan he needed some notebooks for school, wondered where his brother got them. Juan said he knew the place, best prices in town, and would go with him tomorrow. "Okay, catch you tomorrow," Elvis said. "We'll get some notebooks."

They separated, and he disappeared into the darkness.

· 22 ·

Her room was quiet. She sat on the edge of the bed, her head tilted forward, her eyes unfocused, thinking about her world. She had been listening to a radio discussion of how different types of people were affected by diets, but she didn't get far enough along to determine which group she belonged to; that was that. Now here was Elvis. He helped her into her wheelchair.

News about the Big Bad Wolf. She had been hit by some-one on a bike right down the block from the home, and now her leg was in a brace, not healing all that well, and the word was she might not be coming back.

"You know how I'm psychic?" Ms. Oliver said. "Well, I had it on my mind that she had done so many mean things, I wondered if something would happen to her."

Frigid outside. Her window wouldn't close all the way, so she had a narrow red pillow her daughter Janet had made pressed against it to keep out the cold.

Elvis had his own crime story to report. A young girl had been murdered in the apartment above his. It was ghastly, a cut above the customary violence in his neighborhood. The apartment was occupied by a man, his niece, and her two children. The man was on medication for schizophrenia and had apparently neglected to take his medication. Without the drugs in his system, something compelled him to slit the throat of his niece's seven-year-old daughter. He also stabbed the mother and her little boy. Then he tried to kill himself, unsuccessfully as it turned out. Only the girl died.

"I was really shaken," Elvis said. "This went on right above my head. Imagine that."

"I don't think I could," Ms. Oliver said. Oh, how she wished he could move to another neighborhood.

"In my family we had a fat guy who was schizophrenic. He was my cousin. He was like three hundred pounds. He would bang his head against the wall. He got hit by a car."

"It seems you had some unusual people in your family."

Gossip, gossip.

Topic: an aide. Ms. Oliver: "He's nice, but he never stops talking."

"I know, bless us with your silence."

"I asked him the other day, 'Are you talking to someone in China?'"

"Talking to someone in China?"

"Yes, because he was talking so loud."

"I get it."

"We had a Calypso singer today in the auditorium. He was too loud. He was singing 'Matilda,' and it was so loud. If he said *Matilda* one more time, I was going to scream. Fortunately, he didn't say it again."

"I would have liked to be there and see you scream."

She moved on to a new topic: "Some of the people who work here, they always think you're imposing. This one woman, I asked her to pick up my remote. And she came back with, 'You're asking me to do one thing after another.' I could have said, 'Well, that's what you're paid for.' Instead, I said, 'Oh, a pretty young girl like you doesn't mind doing something for an old lady, do you?' And that just pepped her up."

"That's the way to get results."

"It sure is."

"You know, I'm too antisocial. I need to learn to be more outgoing."

"I think you're outgoing."

"That's because I'm comfortable with you. I'm not afraid of rejection. That's what I'm afraid of with a lot of people. I can't handle rejection. I've had too much of it."

He mentioned that for one of his college courses he had to write an essay about how younger people felt about older people. He asked her for any thoughts.

She said, "Years ago, we used to say 'cranky' when we thought about old people. The thing is, they often don't feel well, and so they get short with people. I haven't got to that stage yet. When I was young, there was a lady who lived near us, and everyone said she wasn't all there. But I listened to her because she told funny stories. They weren't true, but they sure were interesting. So I gave her a chance. I didn't write her off. Some young people think old people are passé. They're young and have a future, and old people have lived their lives. Have I told you the story about the tennis players? These two old guys came up to these two young guys and asked them if they wanted to play tennis, and they said, 'Sure.' And they said to each other, 'We'll beat these old geezers.' And the old geezers beat them. Then one of the young guys said, 'I guess they're not too old.'"

Elvis said, "Some young people are not respectful of old people, and some old people treat young people like they're inferior."

"That's very true," she agreed.

"I'm trying to define old age with some of those expressions that you hear all the time. 'The end of the rope.' 'The power is on, and the voltage is low.' 'When you can't carry your own weight.'"

"I'll give you another one. This aide said to me the other day, 'All elderly people have something wrong with their brain.' So I said, 'Young people have a brain, and they don't always use it. I'll compare my brain to yours any day.'"

"Boy, that's true. What I'm going to do is write all these stereotypes and then show how wrong they are. And how, with the two of us, I've been helped by the elderly and how important a part of society the elderly are."

He brought up his back. It had been bothering him something awful recently, from doing physical therapy with the man down the hall and from his years in the food truck. "Sometimes, if I'm having a great day, I won't think about the back pain. But today I was thinking about it. I'm twenty years old, and I have back pain, and I have a daughter now. What if I can't enjoy my daughter because of my back? But I have to provide for her someday, so I have to work. But my back hurts."

"Elvis, you need to get it looked at by a doctor, because you don't want it to worsen and turn into something permanent."

"I know that. I just need to find the time and get some medical coverage."

The baby was a joy and also a stress. The mother was putting pressure on Elvis to provide support, be around, the idea perhaps still stuck in her head that he might settle down with her. When he got cross with her, she would bad-mouth him to his friends. Elvis was juggling a lot of demands on his time.

Ms. Oliver told him, "Elvis, you have to distance yourself from her until you're able to do something financially for the baby. I hope you're not thinking about leaving school. I'm psychic, you know, and I have my suspicions."

"No, no, I'm not."

"Well, stay your distance, because psychologically you can't get too involved. Sometimes when you make a mistake, you make several more mistakes trying to correct the first mistake, and you end up worse off than you were. You have to evaluate the situation and make a decision and then stick to it; don't jump around."

"I know that, and I will." The thing was, he was worried that the mother was going to turn the baby against him, resent him as she got older, the way it had been for him. His mother had bad-mouthed his father so much after he walked out, and Elvis never got that poison out of his mind. He didn't want his child thinking like that, not if he could help it.

Ms. Oliver said, "You know, sometimes when you leave, I want to cry. I worry about all the things weighing on you."

"I'm going to be okay. I can handle this. I've always handled things."

"I sure hope so."

Elvis hiccuped. He mentioned that he was working on

putting away a little money on the side, a few dollars here and there, but money just didn't seem to stick to him. Life smacked him around too much.

"I'm trying to save up money. I have a friend who's a barber. I don't know how long he's been working, but he saved up enough to get his own barbershop. And it's nice and all, and the rent's not too bad. So I'm thinking about that. I would do that in addition to going to college. I want to have a lot of open doors. I don't want to take orders. I don't take orders too well. I'm wondering, How do you get a loan? You have to have something that's worth what you're borrowing?"

"Sort of like that."

"Well, why doesn't everyone do it—start a business?"

"Because if it's unsuccessful, you're in big trouble."

"I get it. You're sort of left holding the bag. I just wish I could save some money. My problem is my generation, we don't save. We get a hundred dollars, and we spend it on jeans and shirts. My mom, she gets a hundred dollars, and she buys ten-dollar jeans and saves the rest. I don't do it. I can't figure out why. The thing is, I want to look good. I want to go down the street and have the girls turn their head and look at me. But I know if I don't save, I don't have anything. For years, I've been trying to figure out why, and I can't do it."

"If you don't save, you don't have money. Money is power. Money gives you options."

"I hear you. I'm going to remember those words: *power*

and *options*. That's my problem. I never feel I have any options. I've got ideas but no options." Elvis stopped, something else on his mind. "I want to ask you, Do you want me to clean your glasses?" he said.

"Yes, Elvis, you're so thoughtful."

· *23* ·

Death hid in every corner of the home. It came out often, eventually getting around to everyone.

There was mystery in every life, how much time was left. But when the end neared, Elvis could always see it in the person's eyes. He knew it as the "death look." Death was on constant standby, the average length of stay of a resident being a little over five hundred days, a year and a half. Whenever someone continued much beyond that eerily trustworthy deadline, well, then you had to wonder, keep both fingers crossed.

He couldn't pinpoint exactly what the look was, it was too ineffable to put in words, but he knew it when he saw it as well as he knew anything. It was some sort of hollow, vacant expression that told him that someone had hours or days until they went to God, or wherever they went.

So when he came in and heard the news, it didn't surprise him, not at all. It was a resident he was really fond of, always smiling at him. She went quietly during the night and soon would live in the ground somewhere.

He told Ms. Oliver, "I knew it was coming. She had that look, the look of death. You know it when you see it, but I can't describe it."

"You've had enough experience to know it," she said. "You've seen a lot of final days here."

"There was this man—he was sitting right over there the other day in the corner—he had that look. He had stomach cancer. He died a few days ago. He was always asking for butter. He said it helped him digest, and so he wanted butter on everything he ate."

"All that butter couldn't have been good for him."

"Yeah, well, like who knows? He wasn't young when he went. I don't think he was done in by butter."

One day, Ms. Oliver was waiting for the elevator, to return to her room. The clangorous doors opened, and two somber men, in dark suits and ties, those thin, tight, surgeon-type plastic gloves encasing their hands, wheeled a patient out on a stretcher. At first, it looked like someone heading to the hospital or a doctor's appointment; then it became obvious. There was no telling if it was a man or woman because the rust-colored blanket concealed the head. Yes, a corpse going out the back door. It transpired like that pretty much every week, another death, another occupancy. She didn't think anything of it. Happened too often.

Just a couple of weeks ago, there was that bizarre streak, four of them on her wing, all succumbing in the space of one week. It was like the dead were beseeching the others to join them, enticing them into the next world. Some of the residents were saying, "They're going like flies. They're dropping right and left." One of them was the Poetry Man, his number coming up. Consolatory calls were made to the appropriate relatives of record—"Your mother passed," "Your father passed"—always couched in the language of euphemism, the crucial word *death* never uttered. The rooms got tidied up, the workers humming to themselves, and new occupants quickly filled the beds.

Recently, another bizarre incident occurred. Now and then, entertainment came right to the floor, in the dining nook, room-service entertainment. On this day the show included a film of musicians performing (a classical pianist, followed by a jazz pianist). Ms. Oliver was enjoying it. She heard the head nurse call, "Come here, I need help." The man sitting directly behind her was rolled away. She couldn't manage to pivot to see what was going on. The home's doctor happened to be at the nurse's station. He was saying, "I'll have to speak to his wife." Curious, Ms. Oliver asked one of the aides what the problem was, and she said, "Oh nothing," and she unwittingly returned to watching the musicians. Only the next day did she learn that the man sitting behind her had died, swallowed his last breath right there in his chair during the film. He had once been a writer, and his wife lived in the home, too, on another floor, often hobbling up with her walker to visit him. Nothing was said when it happened; there was no need to; everyone was engrossed in the entertainment, and death, well, death was not news in the home. It happened that way, quietly, without interrupting the routines of anyone else.

"It doesn't disturb anyone," Ms. Oliver said. "It was their time to go. We all know our time will come one of these days."

Elvis knew that, but it was impossible for him to take such a detached view of Ms. Oliver's inevitable demise. He couldn't imagine her being snatched away. It seemed absurdly improbable. He knew, of course, that when you were in your nineties, every day was one more than you were entitled to by the actuarial tables, a loan of sorts that eventually had to come due. Ms. Oliver was way past that average-stay figure, racking up a lot of time debt.

One day, in a batch of jokes Joyce had sent over, there were a couple of sheets of "Interesting Facts," some of which made sense and some so outlandish you had to wonder if they were actually true, or if anyone could even determine if they were true. One of the facts was that one in two billion people live to be 116, and Elvis suggested that, well, Ms. Oliver was going to be one of those who mocked the odds and hit that big number. Ms. Oliver could only roll her eyes.

But when someone else he knew in the home got that

death look and then fulfilled its promise, he tried to steel himself for the inevitable day he stared Ms. Oliver in the eye and saw it there, when the plausible became the actual.

One evening, Ms. Oliver had a stomach pain she couldn't abide. A stabbing pain, constant; she couldn't tell what it was. Trying to concentrate on something else didn't work. Deep breaths—no good. Nothing would distract her. All she could think about was this pain of uncertainty. Excruciating.

The home decided to send her to the emergency room. It was a regular shuttle, patients going back and forth from homes to hospitals. Many of them were demented patients who benefited little and suffered any number of indignities when they were poked and probed mercilessly in the emergency room, but doctors and nursing homes, what could they do? Few people had bothered to compose written instructions specifying what interventions they wanted, and once they were demented, they were no longer competent to make choices.

When Ms. Oliver first came to the home, she was asked if she was interested in establishing a Do Not Resuscitate order that would prohibit doctors from trying to revive her if she went into cardiac arrest. It was a simple decision for her, didn't take a moment's thought. When her number got called, she wanted to go with her dignity. "When it's time to go, it's time to go" is the way she would put it. "If I get that sick, I don't want to be resuscitated. What for? I don't want to put my family through my living another year or years on some machine. It's enough living this way. I've often thought I'd like to tell those people on dope, 'Don't destroy yourself. Nature will eventually do it for you. So you might as well live while you're young, and then age will do what dope does to you.' When death wants me, I'm ready."

So now, whenever she was transferred to a hospital, she always wore a pink bracelet around her left wrist that said in black ink: Do Not Resuscitate.

The trip to the hospital was just dreadful. X-rays of her intestines showed no blockage, just some diverticulitis. But the hospital played it safe and kept her overnight. It was all very impersonal, very uncomfortable, rousing a stir of anxiety in her. She hated hospitals, yearned for the reassuring sanctuary of her room.

Elvis learned about this incident afterward, and when he saw her the next day they got to talking about death. "You know," he said, "there's a lot of residents here who want to die. One of them even asked someone for a prescription because he said he wanted to die."

Ms. Oliver said, "We were talking about that at the dining table the other day. I've got one new seatmate who has most of his marbles, and so I can talk to him. I said, 'Well, you're allowed to kill other people, but you can't kill yourself. How does that make any sense?' I thought of this, Elvis. You know why Republicans don't believe in abortion? Because they need more soldiers. They don't want them to die young, but to grow up and become soldiers."

"That's a good one. I like that. I think you've got an excellent point there. No one here, though, is going to fight any wars, and I sure see a lot of people here who want to end it all. Some of them are in pain, and others they're just not happy. There's this woman who's always in back pain. She had a stroke, and she's constantly sliding down the chair. She doesn't have the strength anymore to pick herself up. She can't eat well, and she can't do much. 'So she says, I want to go. I want to go.' This other guy I know, he feels alone and doesn't sense he has a purpose. So the guy wants to go. I thought about that, and it must be a hell of a feeling, feeling useless, not seeing any point in breathing for even another minute."

Such a puzzle to him, how a person decided enough was enough, to refuse to live another day, another hour. No longer willing to tolerate the vestiges of what one had become but willing to sample the final unknown.

A few days later, the awful incident: It was after dinner, Elvis doing things late at the home, and he stopped by to visit. Ms. Oliver was sitting in her chair, and Elvis asked if she wanted the remote. She said she did. As he came toward her, she suddenly stiffened and her eyes rolled far back in her head, and it looked like she was about to faint. When he saw the transformation in her, his heart sank. He ran and got water from her pitcher and hurriedly threw it on her face, wetting her thoroughly, drops cascading down onto her blouse.

A nurse rushed in, and finding her blood sugar was high,

she gave her some insulin. Ms. Oliver seemed to become herself again. The doctor arrived and checked her out. He listened to her heart, and it was okay, beating perfectly, but he had her sleep with a heart monitor on, a real inconvenience as far as she was concerned; still, she obeyed his orders.

Later, diagnosing the situation, Elvis thought it was triggered by the demented woman at dinner, her saying to Ms. Oliver, "You dope. You dope." She was at her worst, hectoring Ms. Oliver over everything she did. She said, "You bum, get over there. I own this place." She said, "Move on. That's my husband's place." Ms. Oliver's ice cream was soft, so rather than use a spoon she had put the paper cup up to her mouth, and the woman snapped, "Look at you, you slob. What are you trying to do, eat the paper cup?" Then she slapped Ms. Oliver. She said she was crowding her space. She said she was "touching her wagon." Ms. Oliver said she wasn't touching it and that it wasn't a wagon but a wheelchair. When she slapped her, Ms. Oliver said, "If you do that again, I'm going to hit you in the face." She meant it.

The next night, the bilious woman punched one of the other residents. Before long, she was moved to another room on another floor. Peace would reign again in the dining room.

Elvis actually thought Ms. Oliver was dying, a thought too macabre for him to get his mind around, and he felt a throb of despair. On the night of the awful incident, after he got home, he was incredibly lonely, as lonely as he could remember. He called to see how she was, and she was doing better.

As it happened, Ms. Oliver had hardly any recollection of the incident. She couldn't remember the water being splashed on her face.

Next time she saw him, she said, "I guess now I know what it's like to leave this world. But I didn't see any pearly gates."

Elvis said that whatever she learned, he didn't care for her to learn any more. Wanting to amuse her, get her onto something else, he told her a little story. "You know, my cousin learned how to whistle at a funeral. He had been trying for weeks to learn and was just blowing air, and he tried it at this funeral and succeeded in whistling. Everyone was sobbing, and this kid starts whistling. People were staring at him, cutting him looks, giving the evil eye. His relative grabbed him by the ear and dragged him home. I'll tell you this, he didn't whistle at any more funerals. I'm not sure he whistled again."

· *24* ·

Then, in fact, Elvis's back got worse. It was true Ms. Oliver
had started to worry. He had been scarce lately, not coming
around as often, sometimes not appearing for weeks, not calling to say he wouldn't be there. She felt the sting of neglect,
and she got annoyed at him. It would be like today. He was
supposed to be there at four, but no sign, no phone call. She
sensed the disturbing quiet of something missing. The baby,
college, struggling to satisfy his bills—these were gobbling
up his time—and now the back, all of it causing a panic to
race through his body. He was mightily depressed and irri-
table over the constant struggle, too many events bearing the
same stamp of misfortune. He wondered to what extent the
past owned him. Mooning over his situation, he would complain, "I feel I step out of one puddle into a puddle that's even
bigger. It's like the same shit, different toilet."

Ms. Oliver began to rely on some of the other companions who worked the floor to stop by and do things for her, and she paid them for their trouble. A divorced woman in her fifties had recently signed on as a volunteer at the home, and she came by on Sunday, a convivial woman who worked as a makeup artist at ABC News, powdering the faces of the anchormen. She willingly read stories to Ms. Oliver from magazines, *Vanity Fair* and *Time* and the like. Still, it was not the same. She missed him.

When he did materialize, she teased him, with some trace of actual irritation, that he was treating her like a rowdy stepchild. "Nope, nope, nope," he would gently reassure her. "Not so."

But, abruptly, he would vanish anew. Some mail sitting on the windowsill had begun to curl up in the sun.

Then it was her ninety-fourth birthday, and Elvis dropped by full of good wishes and gave her a card. Inside, he wrote: "On this special day, an angel was born. I've been lucky enough to have this angel in my life. An angel who enforced my motivation which keeps me going. I thank you from the bottom of my heart for all your kindness and always useful advice that you share with me. I want you to know that in my eyes you are more than a friend. You are an angel in the flesh. Love, Elvis."

It was so beautiful, it brought tears to her eyes. She looked into his eyes, really looked into them in a way she

hadn't in a long time, and told him that was such a compliment, and thanked him.

Sheepish, he turned away and just said, "You don't have to
thank me. I have to thank you."

There were offers extended to take her out, from her
daughters, her old friends, Elvis, but she had no interest.
She preferred her smaller world.

In good spirits now, she had to tell him. At that day's Resident Council meeting, a doctor was the guest speaker, and
he had introduced the subject of drinking to the residents.
Drinking as in alcohol. Drinking as in getting tipsy. Ms.
Oliver told Elvis, "He said if any of us wanted a glass of wine
or beer, tell the staff and they would check with our doctor
to see what medications we're on, and if it's okay, they'll
serve us. I thought, if we do that, the aides will be drinking
it. They eat the meals sometimes. One day the Big Bad Wolf
was serving Jell-O, and she put her hand in and took a big
scoop and ate it. Can you imagine that?"

"Yeah, I don't know if that makes a whole lot of sense, giving the residents drinks. Whoa, I've got to think about that."

"It will be like Happy Hour every day."

"Maybe they'll put up a bar, the Senior Bar or something.
People will be wobbling around. At least we won't have to
card anyone."

"I just can't imagine the whole thing. They may end up
having to start AA meetings in the home."

"Yeah, that would be a trip and a half. You know, my uncle died three weeks ago. Liver failure. He drank too much. He was the one who, when I was five years old, gave me these little bottles of beer. I loved drinking it with him."

"Oh my, five and drinking. What a thing to introduce a child to."

"Once I got drunk, and my mother beat the crap out of me."

"How old were you?"

"Like five. Actually, I can't drink a lot. I like a few beers or a shot of whiskey. Black Label especially, if someone has it." He rattled off some other favorites, a drink called the Nut-cracker, which was different whiskeys mixed with fruit juice. Also a drink called Hypnotic that was blue, a fruit blend with whiskey. A couple of years ago, Elvis and his friends invented their own drink. They took a Hypnotic and mixed it with Hennessey. It turned green. They christened it the Incredible Hulk.

Ms. Oliver said, "When I was young, we used to drink Scotch and soda. Supposed to be very sophisticated. Scotch and soda. I just don't have much interest in it anymore. I don't have the desire. You know, I was downstairs, and a resident was smoking. One of the companions said, 'You have to go to the smoking room. There's a room for that.' The resident got very annoyed. He said, 'You can't smoke. You can't drink. You can't have sex. What can you do in this place?'"

"Oh, I know that guy. You say, 'What's up?' to him, and he says, 'Everything's up.'"

"I didn't know that."

Elvis had some good news to report. Espi had helped him find a new place to live, a room in a woman's apartment just a couple of blocks from the home, right on Central Park West, getting him out of the perils of his own neighborhood. Yadira was living nearby, good too. It was a sprawling apartment, with two living rooms, and Elvis's room was just fine. The woman, retired, having put two daughters through college, was the nurturing type, insistent that she prepare meals for Elvis, that he feel welcome to come out and watch TV in the living room, make the place his own. She was charging him just $350 a month, less than he had been paying for his wretched room in Washington Heights.

When he went over there one evening, the improvement was immediately obvious. The elongated apartment was well kept up. His room was small, near the front door, but it had two windows and a cozy feel, and best of all no drunk sleeping outside the door. He ran into the woman who rented it, on her way out, in a long coat and sensible shoes. She was tiny enough to have been a jockey, good-natured, a widow who usually lived alone in the big space. They had a conversation, short and vague. It came up in the exchange that she was on her way to play the lottery, did so twice a week, looking for the big life-altering payday. Apparently, before Elvis arrived, she had been working out her numbers to play. She said, "A few years ago, I got four numbers and won three thousand dollars. That's not what I want. I would like to win several million."

Elvis considered the situation in his mind and nodded. "I hope you do," he said.

He had her rent money, in cash, and he gave it to her, and she thanked him.

She left, and Elvis sat down for a moment to kill some time. There was stillness in the room. His eyes darted to some plastic garbage bags containing his still-unpacked clothes. He was meeting Yadira later. He missed his old hood, but it was time for him to get away from all that, move on. He needed to have fewer distractions, feel he was starting fresh, and he liked being closer to Ms. Oliver.

· *25* ·

The new arrangement didn't last, disintegrating so quickly it barely seemed it had happened. His back ailment worsened. He couldn't get his schoolwork done, found himself falling hopelessly behind in his studies. As he sat in class, the piercing pain would shoot up and down his back, and the math formula on the board no longer mattered. He was unable to drag himself into the home to work some days. Feeling he had no choice, he took a leave from school, and without working as often, his slender income atrophied. He had to let the new apartment go. Once again, he needed to adjust to a new pattern of living. He collected his things—much of his stuff hadn't even been unpacked from the trash bags—and lugged them over to the apartment of his brother's girlfriend, up in the Bronx. There was a cot there they told him he could sleep on. For a short spell, he would stay with

Yadira, who lived within walking distance of the home, but she had two roommates and her place was already overcrowded. It was no paradise, roaches in such proportions that Elvis was convinced they moved the furniture around at night, trying new arrangements, and then there were rats patrolling the block, a guy down the street even getting written up in the *Daily News* for whacking them with a bat, making a last stand.

One thing he was feeling bad about: He had been watching TV last month, and this commercial came on, an appeal to adopt a deprived kid in some Third World country through the Christian Children's Fund. He found he couldn't flip the channel. The next day, he signed up, and twenty-two dollars got him a kid in Zimbabwe. Now he was obligated to pay twenty-two more each month, which he no longer had, and he worried about that kid.

Days and weeks went by, and he barely left the apartment, frustrated at the motions of life. Feelings of despair surged up, and he had to work to shove them back, trying to believe that things would turn in his favor, even though he didn't see how. Yadira and Ms. Oliver helped him forget his pain, but it wouldn't relent. He felt like he was no different than the residents in the home. Noon. One. Two. Three. The hours plodded by, and he more or less did zilch. He would actually check the clock to see if it was time for a certain TV show, an oasis to look forward to. Basically, he pottered around the apartment. Maybe he'd go out and get a juice from the deli, but that was about all. He was losing weight and actually developing bags under his eyes. His grumpy mood was not lost on Yadira, who told him he was giving her a lot of attitude.

People were whispering behind his back about this change in behavior. One day when he showed up at the home, he told Ms. Oliver, "I'm hearing the aides here talking about me, and it's getting ridiculous. They're saying Elvis doesn't want to work anymore. Then that Elvis needs an operation on his back. Then Elvis is dying. Next thing, it'll be Elvis is getting admitted here and getting a bed next to Miss Oliver."

Would his life ever get much better? He had to wonder.

His best friend, Juan, had finally made the decision and joined the navy, leaving behind his plumbing career. Elvis was moping over his departure. The whole idea was repugnant to him. They had talked it out, again and again, and Elvis tried his best to persuade him to stay, go with the trade he knew, but Juan insisted he needed discipline, and he wasn't getting it unstopping drains, being called the Tidy Bowl Man. Weekends, he had worked as a doorman at an apartment house on Manhattan's Upper East Side, but that hadn't done much for him either. He wanted some independence, didn't like being twenty-two and still living with his father because that was all he could afford. Elvis felt Juan had discipline, but that other people had convinced him otherwise, and he warned his friend that being under the thumb of navy officers hardly amounted to independence. He cautioned him: "You're signing away your whole life to somebody else, and they'll make you do whatever they want. If you live at home, you can say, 'Hey, man, I'm not doing that. I'm going out for a walk. I'm going out for plantains.' That attitude doesn't work in the military. They run the show. They can smack you around." Juan had his mind made up and wouldn't buy it. He was stationed in Brooklyn, getting ready to depart for Chicago and then to the Great Lakes for training. Elvis feared he would end up being shipped out to the nightmarish mess in Iraq and finish his military career coming home in a wooden box. Juan was big, all right, and he looked like he could handle himself, but Elvis knew he wasn't a fighter. He had known him since fifth grade, and he could think of only one time he had ever gotten into a fight, and that was to defend Elvis.

Sitting around the apartment, lolling and languishing, nothing to do, Elvis found himself stiff with anger and frustration. No matter what he did, he couldn't dredge up any cheerfulness. He had heard people say life was sweet, and he had to wonder how they could possibly mean it. He even contemplated doing the unthinkable, which was to join the navy, too, and then if Juan was sent to fight in Iraq, he would stand beside him and fight, too. He knew he had to stop persecuting himself for Juan's decision. Ms. Oliver had told him countless times, "Look out for yourself first," and so he shoved those thoughts away.

Brooding one day, sliding deeper into his miseries, he said to Yadira, "I don't know, I'm discouraged as hell. I feel I'm fighting a losing battle. I'm so wounded."

He wandered over to the home and took the elevator to the fourth floor. Ms. Oliver wasn't in her room. He located her in the dining area, listening with some others to Frank Sinatra records, vinyl ones on a turntable, scratches asserting themselves at the wrong moments, but that voice, still that voice. Ritually, he told her, "Allstate's here." He rolled her back to her room so they could talk.

"Put my sweater over my shoulders, will you, Elvis?"

He found it on the back of her walker and draped it over her. The compact television was running with the sound low, images of a best-ever floor polish flickering past.

He confessed his despondency, his potent lassitude, his feeling badly about leaving LIU. "I know it's important," he said, "I've got a lot to learn, a lot about getting from one day to the next. I'm having trouble in that department."

Like others at the home, she had begun to wonder if part of the back pain he lamented was in fact psychosomatic, his yielding to disillusionment. Some days, he would seem so full of energy, no problem wheeling her around. She just didn't know.

Wanting to soothe him, she said, "I'm an optimist, and so I believe things work out. You have to take things one at a time and have a plan. Evaluate each problem, and have a plan to solve it."

"Yeah, I get that. It's just there's so much going on, it's like a puzzle I can't crack. I'm going to solve these things; I feel I can do that."

She stared at him. Oh how much she wanted a happier truth for him.

And then she introduced her own deepening worries. "My eyes have gotten so bad," she said. "On very sunny days like today, it's too much, and I can't see at all."

Elvis grimaced and forced his mind to slide away from picturing what that meant. He said, "I'm so sorry. How good you see isn't everything; you've got to realize that. You're still you. You can still talk and listen and be you, and that's a lot. I don't care if you can see me or if I look like Mr. Potato Head. Just as long as you're you."

She squinted, trying to find his face, not doing it. She hesitated a moment, in solemn thought. "I know I just have to make the best of it. When the television comes on, I can't see it that clearly, not the way I could. That calendar on the wall, I can't see it today. I can't see the clock today. I see you, Elvis, moving around, but not distinctly, you're too fuzzy; you're like a fuzzy blob. I can't see that wonderful smile."

Her faltering vision meant that she could no longer be sure if her bed had been made, and had to ask the question when she saw one of the aides, "Is my bed made?" Wanting the room to look good, and yet having to rely on someone else's eyes to tell her, trust they were telling the truth.

"I feel sort of trapped," she said. "At this age, you do so much less than you used to do, but you still want to do things. Losing my vision makes me feel sad, and it makes me nervous. My body tells me I'm nervous. When I was younger and was depressed, I would take long walks and look at the store windows, admiring all the pretty things on display, and that would make me feel better. But now I can't do that. So I just stay nervous."

"Like I told you, there's still a lot you can do," Elvis said, forcing a smile. "I really don't want you breaking your head over this."

"Okay, I won't break my head."

A couple of pigeons wobbled past on the ledge, cooing.

She quizzed him on his plans.

"I'm going to fill out the form for my financial package to start school again once my back gets better," he said. "I'm trying to go somewhere with the rap thing. I'd like to go to a studio and record something. I'm writing songs. I talked to this guy Joe—he's the son of a resident—about doing advocacy. I'd like to do something to maybe be an advocate for people like you, who need something more, who don't have a big enough voice. There are people here who can't talk much or move, and no one is acting on their behalf, and they get ignored like furniture, like they're a table lamp or a rug or a bookshelf. I maybe want to get into the advocacy business, if it is a business. I don't know, maybe these are very scattered plans."

"But you are going back to school?"

"I want to. My choice is I have to go to school. I have to. Whatever I do, it has to involve school. Like my brother, he's got a business, he's doing okay, but I want to learn the things that will make me really be able to function in the world, and I think you get that in the classroom. I could go ahead and cut hair for ten years and get the money to have my own barbershop. But I don't want to. I want more."

"Well, that's good of you to want more, Elvis. I'm all for that. Sometimes it takes time. You're a young man. You need to have patience. And you need to remain determined. Focus on yourself. Life is just struggling through the days."

She wanted it to be clear that the small repetitive rhythms of her hours were her life but not his, to convince him that there were no easy assumptions about who he could become but that his future was everywhere, stretching onward endlessly.

Elvis scooped up the mechanical grabber Ms. Oliver used to pick up things and fooled around with it, plucking at the laces of his sneakers. He was lost in thought, as if trying to remember something he had forgotten to do. The room was stuffy. It had rained all night. She asked him to turn on the air conditioner. He used the grabber to get hold of the knob and rotate it. Did the job perfectly.

There was a lapse. Here they were, both bedeviled by problems, but they had each other.

Looking to soften the day's parting, he said, "Yeah, Miss Oliver, we got to keep one thing in mind. We got each other, and that's always going to be true."

She looked at him, scrutinizing him, and didn't feel she needed to say anything.

· *26* ·

So sex was going to be talked about at the Resident Council meeting in the auditorium, and why miss that? Elvis, with time on his hands and looking to improve both of their moods, was spending the morning with Ms. Oliver, and knowing it had to be intriguing, sex and the nursing home, they went down and got prime seats in the third row. A bouncy social worker was the host, and she had brought along a film, *Sexuality and Aging*. About two dozen people had showed up, a decent turnout. One was ninety-nine; one was ninety-seven; one was ninety-six.

"Oh, my," Ms. Oliver said, "are they dreaming or what?"

"Dreaming very big dreams, if you ask me," Elvis said.

The social worker stood up in front of the phalanx of wheelchairs. She surveyed the turnout and said, her voice papery, "Our sexuality transcends our biological functioning.

It is an affirmation of being alive. Unfortunately, our society does not view sexuality as life affirming. It is viewed with ridicule and disdain, or dismissed as unimportant." She said it was "easier to view your grandmother in a rocking chair reminiscing than to imagine her having sex." There was no disputing that.

With little additional preamble, the film was put on. Bob, a sixty-nine-year-old man, was interviewed about his interest in sex, which had been latent for most of his life but was strong now. He said, "I'm more sexually oriented and more alive sexually." He said, "I'm a truthseeker. I'm looking for the truth of sexuality. For all my life it's been forbidden territory. But that's not the truth." At the senior center he attended, he said, "most people, it's not even on their agenda anymore. And if they do bring it up, it's giggling and laughing. It's not a subject of serious discussion. Nobody's talking about it. They're walking past each other on the subject. And it's not healthy."

There was some coarse laughter at some of the remarks. There was obvious interest.

Then a woman was interviewed. She said that her sexual desire was not as intense as it had been, but the desire was still there. She said, "Since I don't have a partner, I need to pleasure myself, and I do when the desire strikes me, which is when I least expect it. I would like a man, but since I don't have one, I have another method." She laughed at that, and so did the audience.

Ms. Oliver whispered to Elvis, "Boy, she's telling it like it is."

"Yeah," he said, "and then some."

This was really something, more than they imagined, easily topping the sing-alongs and trivia matches, the usual auditorium fare. They were hearing things.

When the film was over, the social worker said that no matter how old you are, you can't assume you don't have that many years left. She said she had read an interview with a woman who was 111, and who lived to be 122. At the end of the interview, the woman said, "I have only one wrinkle, and I'm sitting on it."

A man raised his hand to comment. Recognized, he said, "I'm about to turn one hundred. I've learned that sex is a normal, natural, wholesome expression of people. All people, unless they're in an insane asylum."

The moderator nodded.

Another man spoke up: "I talked to my doctor about sex. I said, 'Why don't we have conjugal visits like in a prison? I'd like to know how that works in prison and why we can't do it here. If convicts have sex, why not us?'"

A social worker from the home stood up and agreed that that was a good point. She said the institution was struggling with how to approach this issue. "Sexuality is normal," she noted. "It goes on forever and ever. What can we do to allow it to happen here? Your suggestions would be welcome."

The man asked, "How does it work in jail?"

The social worker said, "Well, I've never been to jail."

Another member of the audience had an answer, "It's very simple. All they have to do is go outside the home."

One of the female residents, who was far younger than the others and confined to the home because she was stricken with cerebral palsy, said, "Privacy is key. You have to have privacy. That's the key. I'm only fifty-seven years old. I just lost my husband in March. I have to get lucky. Sex is very important to me. Sex and the single girl."

The social worker said, "I understand. You need to get lucky."

A man said, "I want to say one thing: sex is forever."

The social worker added, "As someone said, you'll be using those parts long after you remember who you're using them with."

Elvis raised his hand, and when he was called on he said, "I've known a couple of husbands and wives who are here, and maybe if we put them in their own room and they can do what they want, that would be better for them. My friend Miss Oliver and me, we think sex is a natural need like washing your face and going to the bathroom. You just have to watch who you do it with."

The social worker said, "It's so wonderful to hear that from a younger person, because there are so many stereotypes. I've had people say, 'Are people in a nursing home thinking about it? Aren't they too sick?' They are thinking about it."

Ms. Oliver cleared her throat and said, "It's a physical need.

Just some people need it more than others. And we have to respect that and take that into account. You shouldn't have to give up everything you need when you come here."

The ninety-nine-year-old had some comments: "I'd like to propose a club. Call it the Sexual Conversation Privacy Club for those who are interested. The problem is, there aren't that many men involved. But we'll try to make up for it."

Ms. Oliver said, "The home has a smoking room. Why not a sex room?"

Elvis said, "Why not have a questionnaire and ask people if they're still sexually active?"

"That's a great idea," the social worker said. "It doesn't have to be about the sex act. It can be about affection."

Then one of the men, ninety-seven, objected: "I think it's out of place. We're beating a dead horse in an institution like this. Sex is just a tickle and a squeeze. But love goes on forever."

A woman said, "I disagree. It's not out of place."

An administrator from the home stood up and said the staff were taking the issue seriously and would look into whether they could have a special room set aside.

The ninety-nine-year-old man had the last word: "It will be a busy room."

Later, Elvis took Ms. Oliver down to the occupational therapy room on the first floor. She had an appointment for a paraffin wax treatment for her hands. She went three times a week, seeking relief from the arthritis, but it was always temporary, something of a tease. The arthritis constantly fought back and, holding the better cards, prevailed.

The therapist greeted her, familiar friends by now from the recurrent encounters. Elsewhere in the room, suffused with busy cheer, old people were hoisting light weights, doing wrist curls, and a man was going at it on a treadmill. There wasn't much conversation. One of the other residents asked Elvis if he could run down to the store and get her a pack of cigarettes, handing him an empty carton with money inside, and he gave Ms. Oliver a kiss good-bye and said he would do the errand and be on his way. She said, okay, she would see him soon.

The therapist sat Ms. Oliver down at a round table and arranged a small bin known as a Parabath in front of her. Hot wax simmered inside, heated to 165 degrees. First her left hand was dunked in the bin three times, a quick immersion and out, and then her right went in. Each hand now bore a thin wax coating like a pair of those sheer gloves dentists wear. Next the hands were wrapped in a towel, keeping the heat on the hands, letting it do its thing. After about twenty minutes, the therapist peeled off the wax. It came off each hand in one piece. Ms. Oliver dipped her hands in soapy water and squeezed on a sponge, having to count to thirty while she did that. It was hard on her flawed hands, and she winced as she squeezed.

Sometimes that was it, but today the therapist wanted her to work a little harder. She put a square Peg-Board in front of her, twenty giant-sized green and red pegs protruding from the holes. She instructed Ms. Oliver to remove them and deposit them in a basket, first do some with the right hand and the rest with the left. She wanted her to extract most of them with her left hand, her weaker one.

In the bad light, Ms. Oliver couldn't even see the board, much less the pegs, all of it an undifferentiated mass. She had to grope for them, and when she had one it was hard to grip it tightly enough to get it to the basket, which she couldn't see either. It was tedious work, a child's task that was nearly insurmountable for her. She dropped pegs. She grasped phantom pegs. Still, she persevered. Steadily, the pegs yielded. The basket filled up. Her weary hands could go only so far, and she had to stop when there were still a few pegs left. That was her afternoon, hearing about sex and encountering too many colored pegs.

At ninety-four, sometimes you had days like that.

· 27 ·

"Brownie, where'd you go?" Elvis said.

Yadira said, "I can't believe Brownie is not here."

Brownie was her dog, a long-haired Chihuahua. Just here. Now gone.

Elvis located him wandering down the hallway, wagging his tail in delight, and put him on his expandable leash so they could take him with them to dinner at a restaurant on Broadway, a rare meal out. The dog was prancing in circles, jumping up playfully, big ears erect. Then he lay down, forepaws stretched out in front of him, twisting his head at every sound.

"His favorite food is cereal," Yadira said to one of the volunteers, scratching the dog's stomach.

"And he loves whole wheat bread," Elvis said. He yawned, lack of sleep catching up with him.

A doctor had finally looked at his back, but the diagnosis was still murky. He said there might be a pinched nerve, but he needed an MRI, had to wait to get that scheduled. He was starting physical therapy. He was working again, doing some companion work a couple of days a week with a man at the home. Not much conversation between them—the man kept forgetting who Elvis was—just wheeling him around. He was still intending to resume school part-time, maybe next semester, maybe the one after that, but who knew.

He had a telemarketing job waiting in the wings as well, the same type of job he had done years ago, calling up people about their creaky credit, their hanging up wordlessly or with a few curses, but he didn't know if he could sit in one place for the necessary hours and listen to the endless rebuffs.

Yadira was of modest height, dark hair, a bubbly young woman of twenty with a sparkling smile and a great laugh, someone who made a good impression right away and cheered you up. She was comfortable to be around. As it turned out, she had her own constellation of ailments. A few months ago, she had tripped on a broken stair coming down from her fifth-floor walkup and tumbled wildly down an entire flight. The upshot was a broken tailbone, two herniated disks in her neck, a herniated disk in her back, and a torn rotator cuff in her right shoulder. She needed to walk with a cane, and now she had developed carpal tunnel syndrome in her right hand from leaning on the cane.

"I'll tell you something really creepy," she would say about her accident. "The month before I fell, I went to the funeral of a friend of my friend. He fell down the steps and hit the back of his head. He went into a coma, and then he died. So when I was going down the stairs, I was thinking: Oh no, this is it. I'm going to bust open my head, and I'm never going to get up again. Life is over because of stairs."

"Two things happening like that close together, it's out of this world," Elvis said.

Neither of them slept well at night, unable to find a position that sufficiently negated the pain. They joked that they both woke up at three in the morning and began comparing what hurt, two people ready for a nursing home themselves. The routine annoyed Brownie, who slept with them and favored a longer night, so there was him waking up too and giving them the look.

"I knew something was going to happen between us," Elvis said. "It had to happen. You were always like the perfect girl. No, I'm not going to say perfect. I don't want to jinx it. You're an intelligent girl. I can talk to you. You're like a breath of spring, as Miss Oliver says."

"How do you like me with my cane? I must be so sexy."

"Now that you ask, that cane does something for me. Girls and canes, I don't know, that's a very good combination."

Their repartee was easy, droll. It was how they often were with each other. Yadira's effervescence worked against Elvis's darker moods, though it could sometimes go the other way. And there were occasions when Elvis was uncomfortable with Yadira's broader learning, her years of college, her more elaborate vocabulary. It sometimes made him feel inadequate and cut off. She tried to convince him of his capabilities, that he had a lot of growing to do. They had their good moments and bad. It was a relationship.

A flat, dull day. They had Indian food at a sidewalk café. The place wasn't very crowded, a few casually dressed couples and an elderly man bent over a paperback thriller, and they were waited on right away. Elvis ordered a rum punch drink, and the waiter, wearing the rumpled uniform of someone still on duty since lunch, carded him. Now twenty-one, he produced the evidence. The food came. Brownie, beside the table, looked up expectantly but got nothing. He turned his attention to a passing poodle, before skulking under the table and curling into sleep.

A bus wheeled past, a new TV series being touted on the side, some show on Lifetime called *How Clean Is Your House,* whatever that was, and one of the two actresses on the advertisement was the spitting image of Espi. "Oh, my God, there's your mother," Elvis exclaimed.

"Whoa," Yadira said. "My mom's been keeping things from me."

"Yeah, really."

On this particular evening, clouds scattering in an untidy sky, the air soaked with humidity, they talked of a future they saw for themselves. Yadira had completed three years at NYU, studying communications, thinking of a public relations career, when she had to take a leave because of her injuries. She wanted to finish school soon, get a master's degree. Acting was her greatest passion, and she wasn't ruling out going into that. Her father, a city cop, wasn't keen on the choice. When she was little, he wanted her to be a pediatrician, but she couldn't make that work. "I have an extreme fear of needles and blood, and I suck at math," she would explain to him.

Elvis, sunk deep in his chair, silently nodded. With their infirmities, they had time on their hands, and they spoke of entrepreneurial possibilities. They worked on rap songs together and were trying to sketch out a play, the plot revolving around young people struggling with their lives, trying to make something happen; they had that one down. They imagined opening a restaurant and bar, thinking they would call it LAB, for "Latin American Bistro," give Latino customers in particular what they like. They'd have test tubes behind the bar, playing off the name. They wondered if they could get investors.

They sat. They ate.

Feelings circled inside them. Yadira felt gratitude for how Elvis had redirected some of her impulses, gotten her to feel the importance of family and what she did for herself. She wore her emotions openly, cried at the slightest provocation. He would scold her, "What are you going to solve by crying? Get over it." When her grandmother died not long ago, Yadira, feeling unmoored, gave up writing poetry, a particular devotion of hers. Elvis galvanized her to take it up again, repairing unaddressed needs in her.

They exchanged glances, lost in the facts of the moment, and she smiled. She recognized that he was hard to change. He would tell her, "This is who I am, these are my flaws, take me for what I am." Some days it was easier than others.

Their lives, of course, were beset with obstacles—the injuries, poor housing, the baby with another woman, something Yadira wasn't keen to talk about—but they were young, resilient, hoping they could sort it all out. Somewhere out there, there had to be a tomorrow.

"I want to have a normal life, like most people," Elvis said to Yadira. "Some people, they have a bad turn in their lives, and they talk about how they remember how good it used to be. I haven't even had the something to remember yet. Imagine that? I want to taste that something—normal life."

He fidgeted with the swizzle stick from his drink, and she ran a hand through her hair, the dog motionless under the table.

Elvis said, "I tell you about this book I'm reading called *Underground Education?* It's full of weird facts, but they're true. For instance, women didn't wear panties for five hundred years."

"Yeah, right."

"I'm not kidding. It changed when they invented bicycles. Girls put panties on because they started riding bikes; it's hilarious. And, I'm telling you, this stuff is true, because they list the sources. You can look it up."

"I think I have better things to do than look that stuff up. Watering a plant would be more important."

"There's this stuff about how people used to blow their noses. People didn't use forks until the 1700s."

"This is so fascinating, I can barely stand it."

It was 8:30, darkness smothering the sunset. Their sore backs reminded them that they had to get up. A bread truck ground past. They moved slowly along the sidewalk. They paused to watch a basketball game played on an asphalt court by teenage boys with sweaty faces, back and forth, sneakers scuffling, the air laced with trash talk, a fast-moving unrefereed game. "Boy, I miss that," Elvis said, staring at a drive to the basket, a pause, and the short jump shot—two points. "I'd like to be out there shooting hoops. I would be, if I didn't have this old-man's back."

Elvis gripped Brownie's leash, and Yadira slipped her arm through Elvis's elbow and clopped alongside him, her cane tapping the sidewalk.

· *28* ·

Fading light falling across the street. Down Duke Ellington Boulevard and into the Jewish Home & Hospital nursing home, where old people with finished dreams came to conclude their living together, a place flush with tedium and small moments. The usual suspects were in the dayroom performing their scripted roles, staring at the passing motion of the street. Someone was working the piano, not well, but not that badly. A visitor was getting his pass at the security desk, carrying flowers in a cone of crinkling paper; one of the residents was in for a treat. The slow and predictable life on 106th Street.

She was in her space, Room 470, the second bed by the window. Same room, same bed. He had not seen her in several weeks, fighting his demons. He rolled her down to the dayroom, where they had some take-out pizza and ginger ale, no Garden of Eden tonight. She didn't want much.

"This pizza's good, have as much as you want," he said, cutting her slice into bite-size pieces, easy for her knobbed hands to handle.

"No," she said when he offered her more pizza.

"No" again for more ginger ale.

"Okay, I see you're Miss No today," he said. "We'll have to live with you being Miss No. Tomorrow you'll probably want an entire pie."

"Oh, now stop that."

She leaned back, let him set to his food. "You know, Elvis, I've been in the home now for almost four years. It's a long time."

"Wow, I didn't realize that. That means we've known each other that long."

She nodded at him, a slight jiggle of her head.

It was left unsaid, but there was little doubt in her mind that her life would not have gone on this long without him, that he had afforded her a renewed draft on living, and it was just as true that he recognized that his life, whatever its uncertainties, had been saved by her.

He had arranged a treat for her tonight. He was taking her to Lincoln Center, where free concerts were put on in the evenings, jazz one night, opera another, the public invited. She rarely wished to leave the home, but this was too good to resist, an opportunity to get herself involved in the stuff of life, and he insisted. The aide had put a nice blouse and pants on her, spruced her up, and Elvis had signed her out, the home knowing she wasn't on the loose, missing in action.

The excitement seemed to clatter after them as they boarded one of the home's vans, Yadira coming along, too. When he went to a special event, Elvis always liked to wear a new shirt, and these days that meant being resourceful. He had managed to pick one up for the concert at a damaged goods store near the home. It was a good-looking blue-and-white striped shirt, marked down to ten dollars from sixty-five, the price reduction based on the fact that some of the stitching was awry. Elvis was only able to come up with nine dollars and had to put the bite on Oliver Lora for the final dollar.

The plaza was filling up when they got there. People were roaming about wearing shorts, striking cosmopolitan poses, looking impossibly young. The three of them sat in a cozy shaded spot behind a snaggletoothed woman with curly wet hair and a man eating a take-out salad and washing it down with a Diet Dr Pepper. Murmurs, munching sounds catapulting into the humid air. Behind them, cars sailed by, the hubbub of the street. The concert was scheduled to begin in a half hour.

Just being here infused her with wonderful memories, all those operas and concerts she had attended in another life. Her vision was fuzzy and untrustworthy, she could hardly make out the white-skinned buildings, but she felt an incandescence. A smile blossomed on her age-textured face. Ah, this world, it still had gifts to give to an old woman.

They chatted easily, as always—events of the day, some nursing home gossip, what and who and when and where, their pullulating topics. She mentioned an embarrassing moment. A friend had given her an audiobook, *The Red Tent*, a novel about a biblical society of women. It got sensual in places, explicit. She was listening to it the other day, and a pretty racy scene came along. The volume was fairly loud, her door was open, and she got a little frantic. "If anyone went by and heard what I was listening to, they'd be wondering what has come over Ms. Oliver," she said. "They would think I'd lost it. I hope nobody heard."

"That's funny," Elvis said. "They'd think there was another side to you they didn't know about."

Yadira smiled and tucked back a wisp of stray hair from her face.

Elvis told Ms. Oliver that Ronny, cutting hair now thirteen years, had bought the barbershop he worked at, putting half down and working out a ten-month payment schedule. He was redecorating it, doing a nice job. He had changed the name from Unisex Salon to Medusa Studio Salon, figuring that sounded ritzy, the sort of place you'd remember and come back to. His mother, having lost her job labeling boxes and noticing a good number of heavyset women in the neighborhood who might want to give themselves a slimmer look, had set up a table in the barbershop and was selling corsets, doing decent business. She also sold fresh-squeezed fruit juices, which moved well in the mornings, people wanting to pump some vitamins into them at the onset of their days. Elvis revealed less of his own ongoing despondency, his own anger at the forces that seemed to conspire against him. He did say he was thinking of trying to sell some corsets himself at the home, a fair number of the workers there carrying a few too many pounds themselves. Maybe that could put some money in his pocket.

Ms. Oliver looked at him blankly and bit down on a smile.

Someone's cell phone rang, announcing itself with the playing of "Hound Dog."

"What in the world is that?" Ms. Oliver asked.

"Cell phone," Elvis said.

"My goodness," she said.

The evening was pleasant, the temperature just about right. Twilight was still at bay on these lengthened evenings. The month was August, the tail end of the summer. It had been cloudy earlier, but it didn't rain. They had never been to one of these concerts before. According to the program, the performer was a young Japanese man named Hiromitsu Agatsuma, and he was playing something called the *tsugaru-shamisen,* a banjolike instrument with a distinctive sound that originated in China and had been adopted by the Japanese. It had a peculiar look and was about three feet long. You plucked the three strings with a jumbo pick called a *bachi.* There was a bass player, a keyboard player, a drummer. The music was a blend of Japanese folk and classical music commingled with jazz, blues, and pop.

The sound was amazing. It wafted out from the stage and seemed to envelop the hushed crowd. Ms. Oliver closed her eyes, not being able to make out the stage anyway, and listened. She felt good and cool and liberated. He had transfixed eyes trained on the stage, watching the musicians manipulate their instruments. Nothing else seemed to matter, just the music. What was wrong with that?

Elvis leaned over and whispered to her, "That sound he plays on that banjo would be so cool on a hip-hop track."

Ms. Oliver said, "Really? I hadn't thought of that."

When the number ended, there was hearty applause. Ms. Oliver said, "I can't applaud, because my hands don't make any noise."

"That's okay," Elvis said. "I'll applaud for both of us."

"Isn't it beautiful?" she said. "I'm really enjoying it."

"Yeah, me too," he said. "I could listen to this all night."

The tribulations of his past would continue to weigh on him, no doubt about that, and his wallet was thin, always scrubbing away at problems. Those were matters for another day. This was now, and he was someone else in this mood, bathed in some new understanding. He tapped his right foot to the beat. The music played and people listened, traffic lights changed and cars pounded past, the city full of action. He was next to her, no distance between them at all, his arm on her chair. He could feel her breath. She was one day older in a very long life. Yes, the years accumulated. A truth hung in the air. Nearly four years with this woman, and they never tired of each other. Someday she would die and enter eternity, but she would never be gone to him, fused as her being was to his. He knew that. Someday, he hoped, he would make her proud. That was fair. He snuck a look at her with interested admiration, and she was glowing, her hair bunched under a hairnet, and then he turned back to the performers. Light was draining from the sky, but the air was still warm, the day gathering itself up. The young man and the old woman, having a good time.

acknowledgments

I am immensely indebted to Margaret Oliver and Elvis Checo for allowing me to experience their indelible friendship. I am also grateful to Espi Jorge-Garcia and the Jewish Home & Hospital for their unfailing hospitality. Thanks to *The New York Times,* where this book originated. Thanks also to Andrew Blauner, my agent, for his ongoing encouragement, and to Paul Golob, my editor at Times Books, for his wise counsel, as well as to Susan Chira and Alex Ward for their support. And, as always, my deepest gratitude to my wife, Susan, and our daughter, Samantha.

about the author

SONNY KLEINFIELD is a reporter for *The New York Times* and the author of seven previous books. He has contributed articles to *The Atlantic Monthly, Harper's, Esquire,* and *Rolling Stone,* and he was a reporter for *The Wall Street Journal* before joining the *Times.* He shared in a Pulitzer Prize for a *Times* series on race in the United States and has received a number of journalism awards including the Robert F. Kennedy Journalism Award, the Meyer Berger Award, the American Society of Newspaper Editors Distinguished Writing Award, and the Gerald Loeb Award. A native of Fair Lawn, New Jersey, he is a graduate of New York University and lives in New York City with his wife and daughter.